In August 2020, Nick Brossoit severe pain in his upper abdomen. ..... being sent to the ER for various tests and scans, the diagnosis was **"Stage 4 Pancreatic Cancer"** and the prognosis: **"Six months to a year."** Nick agreed to Chemotherapy combined with experimental Immunotherapy, and a complex 10+ hour surgery, because **he wanted to extend his life**.

Nick has always had a close, responsive relationship with God. Nick asked, *"Why is this happening? What's going on?"*

God replied, *"It's not about you, Nick."*

"How is this not about me?"

"Nick, you are secure now and you are secure in the next life. ***This is for other people. Your assignment is to share your journey."***

From a difficult childhood filled with heartache and challenges … through a stellar college Football career … to halibut fishing in Alaska … to devoting himself to a career in Education as Superintendent of two School Districts in Washington State … to reaching retirement age with plans of continuing his enjoyment of family, friends and Extreme Sports … to a sudden, terminal illness — Nick's desire to continue speaking peace and encouragement into the lives of others prevails over any fear of death and loss.

"I am sharing what I'm experiencing from a faith perspective, trusting God for the things I don't control" … *"The gift of life was — and is — God's design. It follows that the timing of passing from this life to the next is also His to make, not mine. What is ours is what we choose to do with the life we have been given."*

Meet Nick Brossoit, and learn how to …

"Love the people in line."

A Story of Tragedy Turned Into Triumph

I knew about Nick before he started at the Edmonds School District; he passed school levies by larger margins each time. He talks to people where they are — doesn't talk around them, doesn't talk over them. Nick's journey is one that helps us understand anyone can strive to become the person they want to be. Most remarkable, he is a man who uses truth; you don't have to be religious or believe in a higher power to see that the world Nick lives in is a holy one. The influence he has had on young people and the world, would make any God proud. Nick embodies the power of faith and the power of belief. One of the most beautiful parts about Nick is that he teaches through stories; his anecdotes about life are ways to learn about our own lives. He takes stories of tragedies and turns them into triumphs.

~ **David Quinn;** Teacher, Instruction & Culture Director; founder of allrecipes.com; New York City, New York

Leadership and Passion For Others

Nick and I were both School Superintendents in different Districts in Washington State. Beyond our educational careers, we actually bonded through our mutual love for water-skiing, and then discovered we shared our faith-walk. I enjoyed this book very much because it tells a vivid, real story of someone who came from a pretty tough background, a man with courage, fortitude and faith, who learned to make his life count in meaningful and profound ways.

Two underlying qualities about Nick have seeped through every phase of his life — as an athlete in his youth, as an educator in adult years, and now during his cancer journey — his **skill in leadership** and his **passion for others.** You will want to read this book!

~ **Dr. Chip Kimball,** Director of the International School of Prague, Czech Republic

Virtually Speaking From Beyond the Grave

I had the blessing to share the stage with Nick Brossoit at the 2021 *"Illuminate"* Conference. Nick's story, transparency and heartfelt faith found me thinking about him for days afterward. For believers — and those yet to respond to Christ, who are longing for a message of hope supported by truth — this is Nick's story. He has every reason to shake a fist and point fingers at God; *"Fear, hopelessness, seemingly a lack of justice"* should be his battle-cry — instead, he is at peace, in a place of joy and absolute confidence in God.

Nick is virtually speaking from "beyond the grave" or at least the other side of the curtain. He has already faced loss and death, and yet is at peace. This unique perspective will not be lost on the Reader.

~ **Rev. Frank Colacurcio;** Pastor, Author of *"365 Days"*;
Blaine, Washington

A Real Inspiration, Morale-Booster

I got to know Nick through local gatherings and mutual friends. We were both in Education, and had interesting conversations about our jobs through the years. We often walked a 3-mile route together, and as I got to know him, I realized what a special person he was. His faith, which helped to grow my faith. He would always bring up God and his faith, how He led him through his life; he has always been a real inspiration to me, always boosting my morale.

When I was in the hospital and couldn't talk, not sure I would live, I would text Nick. He would call and pray with me as I held the phone to my ear. I've never met anyone as talented as Nick is, both in his speaking ability and his faith. He is a kind, wonderful man, helpful to so many.

~ **Rodger Teig**; Elementary School Principal;
Lynden, Washington

Not an Ordinary Guy

This is a story you want to read. During the 5 years I was working as Assistant Superintendent at the Edmonds School District while Nick was the Superintendent, there was a child with a previously unsuspected heart condition, who died while running on the track during a PE class. At a staff meeting the next day, after many others had shared, Nick said, *"There is no right way to grieve. Don't be hard on yourself for what you're feeling right now because whatever you're feeling is okay."* It was exactly what people needed to hear. That broke the tension, that helped people begin to breathe again.

Nick's advice is always spot-on, even when speaking extemporaneously; he's an incredibly fast thinker. He usually has analyzed the situation, sifted out the garbage, and reached the point where the solution is at hand. That's discernment.

> ~ **Patrick Murphy,** Ed.D; Superintendent of the Olympia
> School District; Olympia, Washington

A Man of Integrity

I've always known Nick to be a man of strong, excellent character, good faith, highly responsible, living the best he could. Nick is a man full of integrity, courageous about the way life really is. He is not a victim, doesn't look at himself that way. He has been living out this time during this treatment with the view that as he shares this, God will use it however He wishes to use it.

Read this story for the details and the issues involved, and how they play often out in our lives as we learn how to grow in faith.

> ~ **Gary Barckert;** Pastor, *"Sharing Alongside"*
> Ministries; Shoreline, Washington

My Mentor

Nick often speaks in parables or stories — as Jesus Christ did — which is an effective technique, making the purpose of the lesson come to life. This is Nick's story. You will meet a Christ-like man in this book.

~ **Bill Fritz, Ph.D;** Superintendent, Knappa School District; Astoria, Oregon

Unwavering, Natural Faith … It's Addictive!

Many times we hear Christians speaking about how God "works in their lives," and it is hard to understand. But when you hear Nick tell his story, you begin to understand how powerful and peaceful God's "work" can be on your life. He shares a story of our Father's love, he shares how God has been there for him 100%. When you are around Nick, you can sense a peace … a peace so desirable in this chaotic world; and he will tell you every time: "My peace comes from my faith." Nick's faith is inspiring, calming, unwavering, addictive!

~ **Cari Landes,** Sales Representative; Bothell, Washington

Redeeming Our Struggles

Two parallel quotes: *"Christ learned from the things He suffered"* (Hebrews 6:8); and "Nick Brossoit has learned from the things he suffered; he has redeemed his struggles." That completely aligns with how Nick has approached this journey with cancer. Too many people are overwhelmed, discouraged, disillusioned by their struggles. Nick had the ability to persevere through his own struggles — both from his difficult childhood, and now in his battle with cancer — and he shows us that he has learned a redemptive attitude.

If you're looking for a book — either for yourself or someone you love, who is going through challenges — and you want to learn from people who have the capacity to overcome struggles, you will find answers here. This book is a testimony to faith and trust in God (see Jeremiah 29:11). What I've learned from Nick's life and attitude will help me all persevere through challenges I am facing today.

~ **Ann McMurray;** School Board Member;
Brier, Washington

What it Really Means to "Walk in Faith"

The word "peace" embodies Nick Brossoit. I met him when he was Superintendent of the Edmonds School District, and quickly learned what a tremendous friend he could be. When I've needed a prayer partner and a counselor, when I've said, *"I need a Nick Fix!"* — he has always been there for me. I've learned I can feel confident to share difficult things with him without feeling judged; his respect remains the same, and has solidified our friendship. As a Christian, he embodies faith and surrendering. He has helped me have a deeper faith and a stronger walk through life, teaching me "how to surrender and let go" of my challenges, and find the serenity in Christ he has mastered.

~ **Caprice D. Hollins**; Psy.D., co-founder of a Cultures Connecting, co-author of *Diversity, Equity and Inclusion: Strategies for Facilitating Conversations on Race;* TEDx Speaker; Renton, Washington

A Relationship With God Through Life's "Stuff"

Nick's strong sense of God's presence and voice in his life is remarkable, and has given him extraordinary peace. God said, *"This isn't for you, it's for others"* — and Nick has been willing to embrace what God has for him, and to share whatever God has given him in a loving way. If you're interested in a journey that really reflects God working on a life that's been through a lot of challenges yet has become a life that reflects God's presence — showing a relationship with God through all of Life's "stuff" — then this is a good read.

~ **Jim Frey;** School Superintendent;
Lynden, Washington

A Dynamic Testimony of Grace, Love and Power

The intricacies of Nick's journey will touch you and direct you to examine the trials, joys and successes in your own life. His life-story is a dynamic testimony of the grace, love and power of God. I've known Nick over 40 years (we played college Football together). I've been an active spectator of the ups-and-downs in his life, which are communicated so well in this book. Nick's honesty and reflections regarding Life will touch you deeply. Enjoy the read!

~ **Brad Westering;** President/Owner, *"Incite the Mind —*
Inspire the Heart"; Seattle, Washington

A Life Transformed, a Hope Fulfilled

Nick's life story is a picture of true transformation expressed in an irrefutable hope.

~ **Steven R. Ridgway**; Executive Director, *The Northwest*
Network Foundation; Puyallup, Washington

Nick's Book Will Change Your Life

We've all experienced childhood trauma and often carry that pain from unmended scars. However, not too many of us learn Who our Father is — like Nick has, and has come out sharing that with others, like *"bright shining stars."* Nick's emotional story cuts through the doubt and reveals how having a transformational and direct relationship with God can impact the lives of others. Nick, regardless of his own struggles, is a beacon of God's light and love.

I count Nick as a blessing who has influenced my life for over 45 years. He is a mentor, a friend and a spiritual brother for life.

~ **Shelley Bond;** Licensed Massage Practitioner;
Seattle, Washington

Great Life-Story, Inspirational, Heart-felt

This is a must-read, a great life-story, inspirational and heart-felt. You have to know Nick! I first met him while our sons were playing Baseball together. The way he coached and interacted with the kids, it was obvious he was sincere and really wanted to teach the kids the knowledge he had. Nick is a soft-hearted man. Being a cancer survivor myself, this book is very meaningful to me.

~ **Kerry Craig;** Grocery Store Manager;
Lynden, Washington

The Ability to Listen and Be Present While Simultaneously Filled With God

Nick is authentic, and God's handprint is on his life. Nick shares what many great administrators are hungry for: examples from a Christian perspective how to share God's love and wisdom in this world. People need to hear authentic descriptions of how God can work through us. The difficult things from his own life helped shape him into the outstanding leader he became and influenced how he approached people. Nick has the ability to listen, be present with people and seemingly praying at the same time. He follows the leading of the Holy Spirit.

~ **Rachelle Butz;** Chief Technology Officer; Washington State
School District

"Higher Education Meets Holy Spirit Gifting"

Nick is the best blend of "Higher Education meets Holy Spirit gifting." He is bright and educated, yet so sensitive to God's voice and influence. He has the gift of blending the intelligible with the mystical in a way that makes it understandable.

~ **Kurt Langstraat;** Lead Pastor, North County Christ the
King Community Church, author *"GOD101"*,
Lynden, Washington

LOVE THE
PEOPLE
IN LINE

Through the Eyes of My Heart

Nick J. Brossoit, Ed.D

Masterpieces In Progress Publishing House

LOVE THE PEOPLE IN LINE

Through the Eyes of My Heart

By **Nick Brossoit**

Edited by **Jeanne Gossett Halsey**

ISBN 978-1-4583-5355-4

Cover Design: **Kimberly Martinson,** *OutLoudDesign.com*; all rights reserved; used with permission. Photography by **Nicole Medcalf;** all rights reserved; used with permission. Printed in the United States of America by Lulu.com.

DISCLAIMER: This is a work of fact, not fiction; what you are about to read is true. Therefore it has become necessary, from time to time, to change the names of actual, living persons in order to protect their identity and privacy. At no time has any malice or slander been intended, directly or indirectly.

For more information or inquiries, contact:
njbrossoit@gmail.com

TABLE OF CONTENTS

DEDICATION

This book is dedicated to those who read it, in hopes it will draw you closer to God.

ACKNOWLEDGEMENTS

This book would not have been possible if not for ...

- My wife, **Jennifer Vachon** ... my stepsons **Kael** and **Jack Stapleton** ... my son **Kyle Brossoit** ... my daughter **Alisa Brossoit-Baker** ... and my mother-in-law **Lonna Baugher** — for their enduring love and support

- **Terry Smith,** a local entrepreneur, whose business success is only exceeded by his profound faith in God and energy to advance Kingdom work

- A collection of **family and friends** who have been very supportive and encouraging

- My medical team at **Seattle Cancer Care Alliance** and the **University of Washington** — especially **Dr. James Park** ... **Dr. Adam Templeton** ... **Dr. Andrew Coveler** — who have kept me vertical long enough to get this finished

- **Jeanne Gossett Halsey**, my Editor, who knows what she is doing, and who has a heart for God

- So many over the years, who came along at the right time to keep me pointed in the right direction — such as **teachers, coaches, people from the community, pastors,** and **colleagues**

- **Shelley Bond, Rachelle Butz** and **John Steirwalt,** who gave me great feedback along the way, and who are just neat people

■ My BFF **Chip Kimball,** who drove me to and from chemo for months, and has never blinked or turned away in the face of my cancer journey

■ The participants in our Book Cover Photo Shoot (February 27, 2022): **Joshua Grace … Katherine Grace … Fields Howell … Kimberly Howell … Elizabeth Leland … Janae Leland … Jonathan Leland … Hilda Pash … Chad Simmons … Julee Simmons … Gabe Smith … Terry Smith … Jack Stapleton … Kael Stapleton … Jennifer Vachon … Chifundo Vis … David Vis … Duane Vis** — thank you for illustrating the benefits of "loving the people in line"

■ And … you, my **Readers!**

FOREWORD
By Terry Smith

I love this man because I love his heart. A Christian can read this and go deeper in their walk; a non-Christian can read it and discover a real man whose life has always been directed by God. I see God's fingerprints on this book because God has fingerprints on Nick's life. Nick brings inspiration and truth because he speaks straight from his heart, sharing his life the way he's lived it — with difficulties and problems and mistakes — and documenting how God became his Father to help him overcome those troubles, to place them into the perspective that God was always with him, that He would never leave him, no matter what.

Many people get turned off from the concepts of God — through religion, through people claiming to do things in the Name of God that aren't loving — so they throw God out. This book doesn't go through the filter of a church or a religion — it's more of a direct experience of God being active in one man's life.

This book is not about religiosity — it's about a personal relationship with Jesus. If there's anything Nick hopes you will get from this book, it is the importance that each one of us must let God move in to our hearts. There's something about Nick's story that's different. People will say, *"I don't want religion, I want something that's real with a real God."* They want to know God personally. In this book, Nick says, *"Just ask God to show Himself to you."*

When you read this book, I believe you will have a hunger to know God. **Nick shares from *"the eyes of his heart"*** with honesty and clarity, and you will know how to find God too.

Terry
Bellingham, Washington
March 2022

*Terry Smith is the third generation, retired President of **Smith Gardens,** a 120-year-old commercial Greenhouse business based in Bellingham, Washington. Terry is passionate about making a difference in the lives of people he encounters. He and his wife, Carolyn, live in Bellingham, and enjoy their four adult children and their spouses, and thirteen grandchildren.*

PREFACE
By Jeanne Gossett Halsey, Editor

This is perhaps the most unique manuscript that has crossed my Editorial desk; for several reasons.

First: The time sensitivity of getting this book done. Nick had tinkered with an autobiographical book before, shortly after he retired from public service as a School District Superintendent. Several friends read those early raw drafts, and all agreed they could see a great story in there. Then, more recently, a dramatic event took place in Nick's life that changed the dynamic significantly: he has been diagnosed with Stage 4 Pancreatic Cancer. That means there is no longer an endless amount of time for his book to be written, his story to be told.

As I began to learn Nick's story and to better understand him and this — the greatest challenge of terminal cancer — I began to marvel at how he was walking steadily and courageously through it. Perhaps not race-car driving or water-skiing or mountain-climbing, but he is going forward with a calm confidence that is almost eerie ... **unless you know Who is fueling him from the inside.**

Second: A unique thing about Nick's manuscript is that it is roughly only 35% personal "human interest story" or biographical, and about 65% *"God speaking to Nick and through Nick."* You will return to this book again and again because you will not only hear Nick's "outer voice" speaking directly to you, you will also hear his "inner voice" — *"the eyes of his heart."* This has been an exciting journey.

"Exciting journey? About a man fighting terminal cancer?" you may ask. The only reason you might ask that is because **you don't know Nick Brossoit ... yet**. You will learn that Nick has always faced challenges with a determination to win, and this season of his life is no exception. Along this journey, we are also going to meet the Holy Trinity of Almighty God: Nick's Heavenly Father ... his Savior and Lord Jesus Christ, Nick's Best Friend ... and Nick's Constant Companion, the Holy Spirit. **Yes, we will meet God here** too because His Spirit is so intertwined with Nick's that at various times, we won't be able to distinguish who (or Who) is speaking most clearly. Nick is what I call "a true believer," which is saying a great deal. Learn how to **love the people in line** better than you ever knew possible.

Jeanne

Birch Bay, Washington
March 2022

Daughter of renowned missionary-evangelist and popular author Don Gossett (1929-2014), Jeanne Gossett Halsey is a professional Writer and Editor, and has published 92 books, 67 under her own byline. Married to Kenneth Halsey, with two adult children and their spouses, and five grandchildren, she is a member of North County Christ the King Community Church, and often teaches "the School of Creative Christian Writing."

jeannehalsey@mac.com

INTRODUCTION
Through the Eyes of My Heart

God is Spirit, and those who worship Him must worship in spirit and truth.

John 4:24

Enough time has passed. I offer you my truth …
through the eyes of my heart.

Nick
Lynden, Washington
March 2022

Chapter 1: **MY PRAYER AS A CHILD**

I **sat on my bed, pulse racing,** in a degree of shock as I listened to my mother crying in her bedroom, just a few doors down the hall. Through her tears, with a quivering voice, Mom begged Dad to not hit her again. I heard his voice too, not exactly what he said as they exchanged disagreeing words, but it wasn't good.

Frozen, I really did not know what to do. At eleven years old, what could I do? Finally, I left my bedroom and walked down the hall. I knocked on their door.

Dad answered immediately, angrily, and he told me to go back to my room. His face was flushed with fury. Yet I remained there, pleading, "Stop hitting Mom!" Where that courage came from, I still do not know. It was probably not the time or place to be confronting him — at my age and my size, I would not be able to withstand him.

Dad glared at me. At least now, by diverting him, his attention was focused on me rather than on Mom. I turned and went back to my room. If he knew that I could hear him, maybe he would lighten up on Mom.

By now I was also in tears, realizing something terrible was happening, beginning to comprehend nothing would ever be the way it had been before. Lives were being changed that night. All my life, I have lived with images of those years, passing by like a strange yet familiar movie on fast-forward, knowing that the plot and the production were changing. The two people on whom I depended for my stability were not going to be stable enough for me.

In that moment, with clarity, **I earnestly prayed.** I prayed like my life depended on it — because it did. It was a pure, heartfelt, honest prayer, born from the pain of that moment, from the heart of the child I was:

"God, it doesn't look like I am going to have the father I need. God, will You be my Dad?"

That was it.

There was nothing sophisticated, or long-winded, or flowery, or formulaic about that prayer. I could see I was alone … yet **with that prayer, God was there with me.** I felt His presence in my heart. And He has been with me ever since.

Trusting In God

Through the years of my life, I have learned things from many different people, have had a wide variety of experiences, have made both good and poor decisions in my life — but **I will only place my most precious, heartfelt faith and trust in God.** People, even those who are well intended, are simply not capable of loving us, of being there for us in the same way God is. He always will be there.

We can, and should, develop relationships with people, and we should be our best in those relationships — which includes being loving, understanding and showing forgiveness when others let us down. We are not perfect either; we can let others down by our choices and actions, and we must learn to welcome their forgiveness on our journey. However, our "heart of hearts," our most holy of all places inside, must always be exclusively God's.

We so often make the mistake to give that part of our hearts to other lesser or false 'gods." People do all sorts of things to try and fill this place within, to address their deepest needs. I suspect there isn't anything that hasn't been tried. Most addictions, even the "positive" ones, are attempts to medicate those deep pains or fill those empty spaces which each of us carry, absent from a genuine relationship with God.

Many try to pack a "religion of duty and obligation," or head knowledge, into that place, which too leaves their hearts and souls hungry and thirsty. *"Thirsty for what?"* For the Living Water of God's love, grace and acceptance. It's in our **souls** where we feel or sense the living heart of God — it is the part of our beings where we share with Him, for which He — through Jesus alone — fought and won the battle for our lives. I know this ... I tried to live without Him.

If we want, we can share Life with Him. When people speak of "God in us" — this is that holy temple! We need God ... and God wants life with us!

It may surprise people to realize that **God needs us too.** *"What!?"* **God *needs* relationship with His family,** He is always pursuing us — because we are His family. The most important business of all life is to find our way home to Him, to be freely loved by God, and to give that love to others so they too can find the way. Giving God glory is not because God has an "ego need" — it is so people being tossed about in the storms of life will see God as the only Lighthouse and direction to find real life. At our best, we are mirrors of that Light by showing God's love in this world; we are useful at directing the attention of others who are "lost at sea" toward "Life with God."

During our lives, we must keep ourselves — via the use of our gift of free-will — oriented toward God's light and love. It comes from within those who claim Him as their Father, who choose to be in His family. This access, this relationship, is only made possible because of Jesus Christ, the Son of God. Everything else that Mankind tried to reach God failed; then Jesus came to live for us, to die for us and to be resurrected as proof of His divinity.

In a conversation with His disciples, recorded in the book of John chapter 14, we hear Jesus talking about this very same "relationship with God" thing, and explaining how it could happen:

> *"Do not let your hearts be troubled. You believe in God, believe also in Me. My Father's House has many rooms; if that were not so, would I have told you that I am going there to prepare a place for you? And if I go and prepare a place for you, I will come back and take you to be with Me that you also may be where I am. You know the way to the place where I am going."*
>
> *Thomas* [one of His disciples] *said to Him, "Lord, we don't know where You are going, so how can we know the way?"*
>
> *Jesus answered,* **"I am the Way and the Truth and the Life. No one comes to the Father <u>except</u> <u>through</u> <u>Me</u>.** *If you really know Me, you*

will know My Father as well.   From now on, you
do know Him and have seen Him."
John 14:1-7; emphasis added

People today are still asking the same question the disciple Thomas asked, *"How can we find God?"* When we investigate the Bible, we learn that Jesus Christ fulfilled the promises and predictions of the Old Testament, and His life on Earth inspired the New Testament and — through the gift of His Holy Spirit with us even to this day — we can learn how to have real life with Jesus Christ!

We can have an inner Guide in this life, a "spiritual Global Positioning System" (GPS) for those who benefit from a metaphor. His Name is Jesus Christ; Who is still alive and well, and interacting with believers. Our choice is: do we follow His direction, or — fueled by our own egos, our own sense of self-sufficiency — try to drive our own lives?

Chapter 2: **Finding Life In Jesus Christ**

It would be several years before I came to understand that both Mom and Dad were in pain. All of us are wounded at various points in our lives. How we deal with these injuries ... how we interpret the events which caused that pain ... what conclusions we reach trying to make sense of things ... which strategies we develop for coping with all those pains — all of these attempts to make sense of Life shape us. Often we give other people — or events, or circumstances in our lives — the power to shape us, often causing more problems and pain than solving them. It is not until we invite God into our hearts — right at the same level of the pains we experience — that we can begin to heal and be transformed into the people God wants us to become.

Only when our energy and focus shifts to being first about God that we can rise above and overcome those adversities which are such a part of human existence. It is **when the light of God's love in us is brighter and stronger than the darkness in our world that we can be seen by others who are searching for that love, that meaning, that purpose, which transforms and transcends.**

For different reasons, and in ways that each could neither understand nor manage, Mom and Dad being together in marriage was not good for them ... and it wasn't so good for us kids either. If it is true that kids, while growing up, tend to develop relationships which mirror those they saw in their parents, there might be some modeling that is better not passed forward! My parents were married very young, and were quickly burdened with the weight and responsibility of making ends meet while taking care of a growing family. They could not find their way forward without blaming each other for those things unsettled between them.

It is impossible to have peace on Earth when a person does not have peace within. One brings the storms he or she carries into others' lives, and then those relationships suffer ... and the cycle keeps perpetuating. My parents did have some good moments — as Mom shared with me many years later, before her passing — but mostly life was a chore, and they were not a team.

Dad passed away in 2007; Mom passed in 2012. I will share more about my relationship with them — and what I did not have — later in this book. Dad died in peace, at a point where his life had come around in a good way. He and I had a few phone conversations in those final years and were able to reach closure on our relationship. Suffice it to say that when members of our family or loved ones die, it is possible to grieve more for the relationships we did not have than for that which we lost.

Practical Value In Suffering

In hindsight, I have been able to see the things my parents did well, and those things they did not do so well, as parents, as individuals. Working in public schools for over 32 years taught me a great deal about parenting and kids, so even these bittersweet perspectives helped me to better understand my own past and make peace with it. Interestingly, my past has helped me be a more effective educator, and perhaps a better parent and a better person.

There can be practical value from suffering, especially how it effects those who endure and overcome, either knowingly or aware by the grace of God. I don't believe it is "God's will" that we suffer, nor that we suffer from His hand. I do believe He gives people free will, and it is in those painful, misplaced choices and actions that some people make choices which result in great harm. Yet it is also true, as stated, in the book of Romans:

> *We know that in all things God works for the good of those who love Him, who have been called according to His purpose.*
> **Romans 8:28**

Yes, even those really hard experiences we endure from the choices of others! We usually view the events of life from the perspective of this world and our finite lives — yet in truth, in God's view, it's part of our eternal existence, which spans infinitely beyond this life on Earth.

Some years ago, my son Kyle came home from College, distraught from a recent break-up. After listening and empathizing, I got a long tape-measure from my toolbox. I asked him to tell me in inches how long would be a good life. He paused, then replied, "90 inches."

I said, "Okay, show me where you are now by age on this tape." He did. I said, "Point to this exact time, this moment of real sadness of the break-up." He did. I said, "Not wanting to disregard the real sadness you feel now, how does it measure up in the entirety of your life?"

He reflected, "It isn't very big when seen over the whole thing."

Then I said, "Now look at your life from an Eternal perspective, as it exists in God's Kingdom. How long would this 'Life' tape-measurement be?"

He thought, then answered, "It would wrap around the Earth, and go on forever."

I shared how — if we choose God — then He uses our lives here to teach and shape us into our Eternal selves. "As hard as this break-up is now, it is teaching you about yourself, about relationships, Life, and so on, which will help you in the long run. Rather than focus on the pain, ask God for relief, strength and wisdom." In this light, experiences we have which are really hard should be viewed as our "teachable moments" from an Eternal perspective. **God's Big Picture is true reality for us** — beyond our "90 inches" or however many years we are granted.

Questions and Answers

There's a part of me that wishes I could have written my life story differently, but I know that God has used each part of my life to shape who I became, to forge me into the person I am today. God takes our actions — and the actions of the many others who are in our lives — and then is able to discern meaning and purpose from it. I still have some unanswered questions, and I look forward to that understanding when I reach Heaven.

We can choose to learn from the good and bad experiences, and we don't have to forever be the victims of the actions of others. God can help us understand and construct something meaningful from even the ugliest experiences of Mankind. Clearly, given what some survived growing up, we might want to script a different set of parents, and we must certainly do better as parents ourselves, so that we write the story of our children's lives better. Still, there is a point where what our parents did (or did not) matters less than the choices we make for our kids, and the choices we make for ourselves.

The most important choice any of us must make is the one to invite God into our hearts, in a very real and personal way. This is the only choice possible because of the Bridge which God provided to re-connect us to Him: the gift of His own Son. In Biblical terms, this is the New Covenant which God gave us. **The life, the death, the resurrection of Jesus is our way to Life … and the presence of the Holy Spirit is our Guide.**

34

Chapter 3: "Survival of the Fastest"

F amily life in my early years, as the youngest of six children, had both benefits and disadvantages. With so many kids, there was always someone with whom to play. My sisters, being older, were often tasked with looking out for me, and I am thankful for the gifts of the time we spent together.

Family meals were always a production; and if there was some type of dessert with dinner, one had to move quickly as "survival of the fastest" was certainly a fact of life around our dinner table. Each of us had our own laundry pile, and were responsible to fold our own clothes when they were clean.

Even discipline was organized in our house. When there was some event which caused Mom to issue spankings, she would pull out the kitchen drawer filled with large utensils and begin shaking it, over and over, so that everybody in the house could hear the ominous sound. When we heard that drawer shaking, all my brothers and sisters would scramble for their respective bedrooms. Then Mom would select a wooden spatula for a paddle and would begin making the rounds of the bedrooms, oldest child first. A door would open, a smack would sound out, a cry would ensue ... and then another door would open, another smack, another cry, all the way down the line. Her approach was, *"If nobody confesses, all the kids will get spanked, just to be sure to get the guilty one."* For some reason, she rarely opened my bedroom door — I don't know if she had run out of energy, or if she thought I had suffered enough just listening to her spank my siblings. Or maybe she figured I was not the offending child, and she wanted to spare me. Whatever her reasons, I was always glad to have her pass over my door.

Mom was born into a large family; her parents had come from Germany. Dad was born into a smaller family; his parents came from France. They were both first-generation Americans. They met while in High School, but neither completed any education beyond that point. Dad served in the Navy for awhile, but soon after that, they were married, and had kids on the way; he became a professional hairdresser, and eventually had his own salon.

My five siblings were Jan (born 1949) ... Doug (1950) ... Sam (1951-2021) ... Renée (1952) ... and Scott (1954-2020); there was a five-year break, and then I was born in 1958. At birth, I was nearly 12 pounds, which couldn't have been an easy delivery. After my difficult birth, that's when Mom started smoking and drinking.

I can't honestly relate to what it must have been like for her to give birth to a baby that large, with no Caesarean-section procedure to help hoist me out. I've asked women who have given natural birth to large babies, and they just roll their eyes. Mom said I was always hungry, so they cut the tip off a baby bottle's nipple and would mash up cereal into the formula, just to hold me over.

Mom liked to joke and tease a lot. She was not a complicated person: if she liked you, you were in — but if she didn't, you were out. If she loved you, she showed it — and if she didn't ... well, you had best been walking in the cross-walk when she was driving or she'd as likely run you down.

Mom and I used to play Cards together, games where you could earn points; those games seemed to go on for days. This was our special connection, one both endearing and enduring throughout the years we shared.

Before my parents' relationship came to an end, we did normal family things, celebrating birthdays and holidays together. I recall some exciting Christmas mornings, everyone running to see their gifts and toys left near the tree by Santa. We'd notice the half-eaten cookie on the plate that Santa had (allegedly) snacked on, and whatever was left of a carrot his reindeer had nibbled on during their stay at our house. I never questioned Santa's existence until, much later, one of my brothers informed me that Santa did not exist — it was really Mom and Dad who played his role. That really bothered me: *"If Santa isn't real, then what else have I been told that might be untrue?"*

I must confess that in my two marriages (both with young kids), I have participated in this "Santa myth" rather than take on the battle with my wife. Relationships are negotiations, and it's difficult for either party to establish absolutes, particularly when it comes to raising kids. If you are heading toward being a parent, or already in the process, be sure to have these conversations early as a couple and get some of these points dialed in to agreement. When in doubt, compromise … or fight out of love, as opposed to having intellectual or idealogical sword-fights.

The Bomb Shelter

We lived in the small town of Ephrata, in central Washington, during my earliest years. Given that there were eight of us and we needed more space, my parents added a family room to the back of the house. They also constructed a "fall-out (bomb) shelter" below the addition, due to the political fear of nuclear war which impacted our lives, accentuated by "the Cuban Missile Crisis" (1962). My parents even had us do emergency evacuation drills to the bomb shelter, which was stocked with bedding, food, water, even an old bike which ran a fan/vent system to pull fresh air into the underground space from the outside. I asked, "How can it be okay to breathe air on the inside from the air on the outside where a bomb has dropped?" I never got an answer that made sense to me. We never needed that shelter for nuclear war — most of the explosions that happened in our family came from within the house, not from external threats.

Our house backed up against a hill in Ephrata where a young boy could explore, build forts, ride bikes without helmets, collect bugs, throw rocks into the canal which provided irrigation to the area, and basically just go outside and play, without fear of abduction or being hit by passing cars. Dogs rans free, and everyone on the block knew everyone else, so it was no big deal for kids to run wild in the neighborhood. There was enough space in all the yards of the houses that we could easily play games with neighbor kids — Tag, Hide and Seek, or Kick Ball down at the end of the street.

Childhood Adventures

There was one time when I caused a bit of a stir. There was an ant-hill behind our house; I decided to roast the helpless critters. I was using gas from an open can of gas (probably fuel for a lawn-mower), but my aim wasn't very accurate. I poured the gas on the ant-hill and set the gas can a few feet away, spilling gas inadvertently. I lit the fire ... and then the flames started moving back toward the open can of gas. Being a kid, I kicked the gas-can further away, causing fresh gas to spill out in a fan pattern.

By now the flames were spreading faster, and ... let's just say that a couple of fire-trucks later, they were able to put out the grass fire which had spread on the side of the hill. I got a good scolding from the fireman about playing with fire; but I think they spent more time querying my parents about how I was able to get matches and a can of gas in the first place. No extreme harm was done to people or property that time, although I'm sure the ants would have preferred otherwise.

Other than once sneaking some of Mom's cigarettes and trying to light them under the bridge that spanned the canal, I never again used matches in my youth. My pyrotechnic career was short, and limited to those events.

Also, I never smoked beyond that one experiment, and could never see the attraction of smoking. Once in my 20s, I dated a girl who smoked; regardless of her personality and other attributes, kissing her was like licking an ashtray, so I ended it ... and she likely never understood why. Maybe I should have told her, but I was still pretty immature. It was like being in one of those *"Mr. Potato Head"* relationships where you want to move parts of the other person around a bit, then realize there are too many things you want to change, and you really cannot live with that combination. Either we accept people for who they are, or punt and move on.

Later in life we learn about accepting other people for who they are and stop trying to change them. That is God working in us and in others; it is not our work to do in others. Praying for others and loving them is really the best approach, all things considered.

"Kangaroo Legs"

Another pivotal childhood moment happened when I was about 8 years old. My older brothers tied my hands behind my back, and told me I could not get out of their tie-up. I was determined to show them I could, so I jumped with both feet into the air, swung my arms under my feet — clearing one leg just fine but catching the other as I fell. Gravity does that, you know. This resulted in the breaking of my left femur, and me ending up in traction in the hospital for several weeks. Because of the complexity of the break, I went home in a body cast.

My brothers felt awful for their part in the event; I don't think they intended or wanted that outcome. Still, I got a lot of attention and pretty much had them as my personal servants, which more than made up for it. Due to the body cast, I could not reach my own bottom; there was a "trap-door" in the cast which allowed for those functions. I think it was Mom who stepped up to help me with that business — the things we put our own parents through!

The doctor, Wayne Piper, who managed my broken leg had also delivered me at birth, and had delivered most of my siblings. Ephrata was a small town, and he was the doctor for many. Dr. Piper was an interesting person and had lived an interesting life. Most of the younger people — perhaps even some of the older ones — thought he was "cool." One night at the local motor-sports track, he pulled off the track right in the middle of a race, diverting his race-car off the track onto the street, driving instead to the hospital to answer an emergency. The announcer even told people Dr. Piper had been called to the hospital. Later that same night, he returned, still in his race-car, and joined in other events.

After I was allowed to leave the hospital, Dr. Piper made a special point of talking with Mom about the seriousness of this type of bone-break, especially for someone my age. Apparently, due to the growth plates, if I did not get physical therapy, there would be a good chance I would never be able to run again, might even have problems walking. The traction treatments in the hospital and the body cast at home were especially intended to address the eventual bone length issues which could develop over time. He did his best to set the bones correctly, but there could be problems with the long-term recovery.

We were a poor family, and certainly did not have the money for physical therapy. Mom took an old pair of jeans, cut the legs off, sewed the truncated ends closed, filled each side with rocks, and then tied the two loose ends together. Every day, she would make me do the leg exercises Dr. Piper had prescribed — it was physical therapy at home. She made me exercise. I would not have pushed myself as much as she did, but she was relentless, and amazing. All the while she was working my rehabilitation, she was also taking care of five other kids, looking after Dad, the house, even employed outside the home part-time. Thanks to her diligence, eventually I was able to walk and then run quite well.

My recovery was so complete that I looked a bit like a kangaroo: I had a normal-size body and arms, with oversized legs. I was so active that, by the time I was 10 — and until organized Football started in the seventh grade — I used to recruit older siblings or kids from the block, and set up games. I lined up parallel garden hoses, creating a running chute in the yard. The other kids would take turns "being the defense," trying to stop me as I carried a football and tried to run through them, over them, or past them, all within the boundaries of "the chute." After I wore out one person, I recruited another and so on.

My greatest asset was my leg strength. It was the best feeling to outlast all of them, especially when they were older and bigger; it was quite satisfying to, more often than not, succeed in that play. I also loved the feeling of being totally exhausted from all this activity, knowing I had really challenged myself somehow. Playing Sports was so much more fun than simply watching them; to this day, I am not much of a fan of "watching" — I would rather be "doing."

Chapter 4: **God In the Turmoil**

Not long after the fighting escalated between Mom and Dad, one afternoon my sister Renée saw me coming in from playing out back, and she stopped me on the porch. She had a serious, sensitive look on her face — she told me that Mom and Dad were getting a divorce.

I wasn't quite sure what all that meant, but I did understand they would not be together any more. I admit there was a young sense of relief that the drama, perhaps the trauma, in the house would stop. I had no idea what Hell would soon be released toward our family. It almost became like scenes from *"The Lord of the Rings,"* where the Wraiths would be set loose against innocent people. Only in this case, they would be going after my siblings, my parents, and me.

My family was born into the Catholic religion; we were all baptized and raised as Catholics, which included attendance at the local Catholic Grade school, *Saint Rose of Lima*. This is what I knew; it seemed normal to me. We would go to church, learn about God through the lens and interpretation of that religion. I wasn't too sure about some of the practices, not too sure about some of the people I met there either, but I knew God.

One day, a priest came by the house and told us that, because Mom and Dad had divorced, none of us would be able to attend the Catholic church anymore. This did not seem quite right to me. *"What have I done to deserve this?"* Yet, while the church was cutting us off, I never felt rejected by God — **I had asked Him to**

be with me, and He was. He was still with me in all of this turmoil. Actually, based on some of the people I had met, I wasn't sure God was attending that church anyway.

Learning Love and Respect …

I had known various people, including priests and nuns, who would come and go through the Catholic church and school, but there were only two — one priest, and one sister at the school — who actually seemed to carry the love, grace, compassion, light, and understanding of a living and loving God. Only two, of all the people I met. I am pretty sure I met and experienced God through Father McDonald and Sister Stella Joseph.

At *Saint Rose of Lima* grade school, I had fun and I had friends. I was good at Sports; we had all been together since kindergarten. Fifth grade was with Sister Stella Joseph, who taught us many skills and subjects, but also taught us about grace and compassion. One day, a classmate named "John" came back from lunch with "a peanut-butter smile" on both cheeks; an hour after lunch, he still lacked awareness that he had eaten his peanut-butter sandwich with too much exuberance. Some of us were laughing, having great fun teasing John, making funny comments like, "Hey, John, how was lunch?"

Sister Stella quietly called John to her desk, whispered something to him, and he quickly left the room. When he returned, his face was washed. During the time he was out of the room, Sister Stella just looked at us. She was not angry, nor she was smiling; there may have been a look of disappointment on her face. Even now I remember what she said to all of us: *"And if you are John?"* We were silent. Her words were loving but they were piercing too, to that deep place inside each of us where we sort out what is right or wrong.

We respected her. We loved her as our teacher. She was awesome. We had treated John without dignity or respect. Sister Stella treated everyone with dignity and respect, even we who were teasing John. In that moment, she pulled our hearts into hers, and into John's ... and we understood. Jesus does this with us now, just as He did so many years ago in Person in our world. When we are walking in the Spirit today, we can be like Him in the way we treat others.

... and Disdain and Disrespect

I made it to the sixth grade at *Saint Rose of Lima* ... and I ran into Sister Veronica. She was my sixth grade teacher and was in charge of the whole school. She was nothing like Sister Stella. She was mean-spirited, strict beyond any reasonable boundary, and I am not sure she even liked kids. Sister Veronica and I collided immediately.

I was the leader in my peer group, and none of us liked her. Often I would try to talk with her about our childhood concerns, but with no success. This resulted in me getting in trouble often ... and Mom's phone ringing just as much. After the first two weeks, Mom decided that "flight was preferable to fight" with Sister Veronica, and I was abruptly pulled out of private school and transferred to sixth grade at a public school.

How did that happen? One day we kids had been outside at recess and — even after she directed me not to do it — I tossed a rock in Sister Veronica's direction. She had the disposition of a constipated wild-cat. She was so harsh to me and the friends whom I had developed through five successful years at that school. Coincidentally, the rock-throwing incident was about the same time as the bottom was falling out at home; I am sure to some extent that I was displacing some of my frustrations at her.

At age 12, one lacks the insights to fully understand all the emotions swirling about inside, and lacking the language skills and emotional intelligence to share in a more constructive manner, I was doing what a troubled boy does: simply acting out. While I was "successful" in expressing via my behavior my displeasure for her, I did not comprehend the power of her authority over my young life. She actually did carry a ruler, and would smack us on the back of the hand in class.

Sometimes, for more serious offenses, we would be sent to see the priest, to make a confession. "Confession" is when a "sinner" (me) tells the priest — who is on the opposite side of a curtain — what we have done wrong; we then ask for forgiveness; and then the priest assigns some "penance" (a means of restitution) to do as a follow-up. Most often in those days, penance was saying prayers.

Now I am not sure about the concept of assigning prayers as a consequence for bad behavior, but that's how it was done. Also, I am not sure I ever understood the different sides of the curtain: I knew who the priest was, and he knew who I was; it was a small school, after all, and he could easily recognize our voices. I think the idea was that the curtain created some kind of connection between me and God — or maybe it was a barrier between me and God? — or maybe the priest was supposed to be acting in the stead of God, and we were pretending we were not really talking to the priest whom we knew but somehow "to God"? It was confusing. Symbolism doesn't always work on a realist.

After the rock-throwing incident, I was sent by Sister Veronica to see the priest in confession ... except I wasn't sorry for what I did; I actually was quite clearly expressing my feelings and views towards her. I even thought I was justified in my actions, and wondered why **she** didn't have to go see the priest and confess for being so mean to everyone! I do think the priest was holding back some laughter when he heard all this during my confession, which consisted of me carefully describing the situation from my perspective, and the disdain I had for Sister Veronica. I was thinking: *"Finally! Someone with authority will understand, will see my side of the incidents, and help."*

I will never know to what extent he did — or did not — agree with my views, because confession is not a conversation. He listened; he stated I should not toss rocks at Sister Veronica; then showed no lenience in the assignment of my penance. As a result, I developed sore knees from endless *"Hail Mary's"* and *"Our Father's"* ... but now it was all coming to a close. I remember looking out the windows of "Nelly Bell" (our old Chevy station wagon) as Mom drove us out of the parking lot and away from that school, thinking, *"What is going to happen next?"*

The next day, I was escorted to a sixth grade class at *Parkway Elementary School,* the local public school. It was a typical, traditional classroom. I heard rumors of "hacks" given to students who misbehaved. There were no nuns, no priests, no confessions. Once I saw a teacher actually lift a desk — with the student still sitting in it — in order to realign the legs of the desk with the markers on the floor. After witnessing that, I thought, *"It's best just to stay within myself ... and, for sure, keep the legs of my desk where the assigned marks on the floor may be."*

I did not know any other students. Everyone I had grown up with were at the other school. I missed my friends. In this classroom, I was invisible. It was only at recess, when it came time for the daily game of Football, that I bloomed. I was good at that sport; my skills became a way for me to establish myself, and even gain a higher place in the social pecking order with other students. Nobody really knew me, nor the pain I was enduring in my life. There was relief for me in the play of recess; in the middle of a game, nothing else mattered.

Chapter 5: **The Nature of Evil**

Before I share more of the pain behind the story, especially about my parents getting divorced, I need to establish a Truth:

There is Good and there is Evil in the world

God is good, yet evil things happen to people. When bad things happen to people, it is a function of the terrible use of free will which all people are given — or, with the influence of evil, perhaps a mix of both. Understand that just as God exists, so does the Devil exist; this is detailed in the Bible.

Many Christian and religious groups don't want to recognize this, or prepare people for the butt-kicking, heart-breaking spiritual warfare we all are born into. Jesus was born into a lost world. He was hunted by Evil (Satan) when He was still a baby — in so much danger that God, via an angel, warned His parents to flee before the evil, prideful ruler issued the order to have all children under age two to be savagely killed; Herod's intent was to wipe out the "new king" (Who was, in fact, Jesus Christ, Who had just been born; see Matthew 2).

How do we confront or face Evil? Imagine if we hear a knock on the front door, and open it to see the Devil standing there, breathing fire, horns and pitch-fork and all. Most likely we would slam the door and call 9-1-1! But we know that Evil is not like that — Evil is subtle and deceptive, sneaks up on people. At times, Evil comes as the proverbial "wolf in sheep's clothing"

— we let it into our lives because we don't see the danger, at first.

> "[The Devil] was a murderer from the beginning, **not holding to the truth for there is no truth in him.** When he lies, he speaks his native tongue, for **he is a liar and the father of lies."**
> **John 8:44;** emphasis added

Evil does not play fair or show mercy. It does not ease up on the weak or vulnerable out of a sense of fair play. Evil tries to kill and destroy the hearts and hopes of people, to lead them astray from God, to distract them and attract them to other false gods.

> Be alert and of sober mind. **Your enemy, the Devil, prowls around like a roaring lion, looking for someone to devour.** Resist him, standing firm in the faith, because you know that the family of believers throughout the world is undergoing the same kind of sufferings.
> **1st Peter 5:8-9;** emphasis added

The closer we move toward God in our lives, and the more we help or lead others in God's way, the greater the activity and intensity level of Evil. The goal of Evil is to get us unsettled, to plant doubt and confusion. Evil targets us, and most often, we are sitting ducks. On our own, we won't win these duels — but we can and should audibly call on and claim the Name of Jesus to resist and overcome Evil! [1]

Evil thought he knew Jesus really well, how to massage His ego, how to appeal to His needs, and tried

---

[1] See Ephesians 6:11; also Matthew 4:1-11

to seduce Him. Satan hasn't changed his methodology in the least: he still tries to lure us with some shiny penny on the sidewalk and try to get us to step off the path that leads to the Streets of Gold as God's promise of Life. [2]

Sometimes Evil can come in the name of "religion" or even under the pretense of "being from god." Other times Evil comes through other people who, in those moments, are not acting on behalf of God or our best interests. [3]

Just as some people yield their lives to the positive influence of God via the Holy Spirit, there are others who, either knowingly or unknowingly, are being influenced or used by forces of darkness to attack the hearts of others — and they specifically attack those who have been given access to God's Kingdom through our Lord and Savior Jesus Christ. Sometimes people act based on their own interests, regardless of how it impacts others; Evil doesn't even have to exert pressure on them because they have already allied themselves with him.

People can be instruments for Good … and people can be instruments for Evil. I'm not saying that people are evil, but they can by used by Evil to cause harm to others. How? Often they make poor choices of their own free will; often they are only looking out for themselves, regardless of the consequences to others; and sometimes their actions are the influence of evil spirits trying to use them to hurt others.

---

[2] See 2nd Thessalonians 2:6-12

[3] See 2nd Corinthians 11:3-4

Evil Can Be Subtle

Satan can be subtle. He can trick a good person into doing or saying something evil, resulting in harm to others. A perfect example is found in Matthew 16, where, at first, Peter's opinion of Jesus is magnificent and inspired by God ... but a few short verses later, Peter falls into a human perspective, and Jesus rebukes him for speaking untruth:

When Jesus came to the region of Caesarea Philippi, He asked His disciples, "Who do people say the Son of Man is?"

They replied, "Some say John the Baptist; others say Elijah; and still others, Jeremiah or one of the prophets."

"But what about you?" He asked. "Who do you say I am?"

Simon Peter answered, "You are the Messiah, the Son of the Living God."

Jesus replied, "Blessed are you, Simon son of Jonah, for this was not revealed to you by flesh and blood, but by My Father in Heaven." ... From that time on, Jesus began to explain to His disciples that He must go to Jerusalem and suffer many things at the hands of the Elders, the Chief Priests and the Teachers of the Law, and that He must be killed, and on the third day, be raised to life.

Peter took Him aside and began to rebuke Him. "Never, Lord!" He said. "This shall never happen to You!"

Jesus turned and said to Peter, "Get behind Me, Satan! You are a stumbling block to me; you do not have in mind the concerns of God but merely human concerns."
Matthew 16:13-17, 21-23

Peter loved Jesus and really, really cared about His welfare. He didn't intend to interfere with God's ultimate plan for the life of His Son — which was to become the Sacrificial Lamb Who came to take away all the sin of the world for all time — but in his natural self, Peter didn't want His Lord to die! He tried to talk Jesus out of the suffering, the death and even the resurrection which Jesus had to do to complete His mission on Earth. Peter was not Satan — but in that moment, perhaps even thinking he was being supportive and protective of Jesus — Peter was actually being manipulated by an evil force to try to throw Jesus off track.

Jesus did **not** say, *"Peter, stop trying to protect Me!"* Jesus **did** say, *"Satan, get out of here!"* Jesus correctly identified the slippery, sneak attack of Satan, actually infiltrating one of Jesus' best, closest friends. Even a disciple of Jesus was, at times, in the right light and, at least in that moment, was not.

Every one of us needs to understand that our **only** chance of resisting and overcoming Evil is by staying connected to the closeness and power of God in us:

*"I am the Vine; you are the branches.   If you remain in Me and I in you, you will bear much fruit; **apart from Me, you can do nothing."***
John 15:5; emphasis added

This is not a one-time, set-it-and-forget-it decision. This is not depending on what is happening around us. Connecting with God can be a moment-by-moment choice and awareness. We should not get cocky, or smug, or confident in ourselves — test the thoughts and feelings we have, asking, "What is my real motive for the things I want to say or do?" and submit everything to God's Light by quick prayers. The Holy Spirit is **always** watching, always listening, and always willing to reach out to us:

Submit yourselves, then to God.   Resist the devil, and he will flee from you.   Come near to God, and He will come near to you. ...

Humble yourselves before the Lord, and He will lift you up.
James 4:7-8, 10

Flowers and weeds grow together. We all have flowers and weeds in us, and at times we act more like one than the other. How we live our lives toward others is mostly a product of the choices we make, the "gods" who don't give life but we serve them anyway — or, when we find Jesus and invite Him in, we begin to serve God, the real God. When we come to God, He sees all our flowers and weeds, and He takes over the process of removing the weeds and nourishing the flowers. 4

---

4 See 1st John 1:5-10

Our allegiance to the Light (God) — or to Evil — shows up in our hearts, and then in our lives in the actions which follow. The fruits (or products of a Holy Spirit-led life) are evidence of a person walking with God — and conversely, the results of one who is being led around by other forces (Evil) usually leads to someone doing anything they can to medicate their pain-filled hearts, to fill the emptiness they live with inside, which often results in using or hurting others.

People's lives are often wounded early, such as childhood; this is an attack against innocence. How we react to those wounds will determine a great deal of what follows. Keep this in mind — or rather, keep this Truth in your heart — as you continue reading my story.

Chapter 6: **HOME LIFE REDEFINED**

After the divorce, Dad had already moved out and, very quickly, he remarried. He made a few attempts to connect with his kids, but mostly, I think he was relieved to be rid of Mom and their strife. Some of the older siblings were moving out on their own, and he didn't seem to want to be bothered too much with those who remained at home.

To compensate for my lack of a "father figure" or a "man's influence," I pressed in to listening to Coaches and other adults, sort of adopting them as responsible adults in my life who could give me any kind of guidance. Mostly, they were Little League Baseball coaches, or Ski Team coaches, the fathers of my friends, Cub Scout advisors, teachers, school coaches, even the men for whom I worked part-time. They never knew I was using them this way, but I did ... and maybe God did, on my behalf. God remembered my childhood prayer, and continued to make good on it. Young men need older men to show them the way, in a good way!

Mom was deep into depression, using alcohol too much, constantly having "dates" to numb her pain and distract her broken heart. By this time, I was 12 years old, and most of my older siblings had moved out of the house. Life for me was school, sports and, well, taking care of Mom.

Many times she would stumble home from an evening spent at the bars, too drunk to take out her own contact lenses. I used a small optical suction cup designed to remove her contacts, so I could put her to

57

bed. She seemed oblivious to the backwards relationship, with me looking after her.

Once, a man followed her home from the bar; he tried to enter our house so he could follow her to her bedroom. I met Mom at the door and moved her inside, then turned around to meet the guy outside the door, grabbing a baseball bat to reinforce my refusal to let him in. He resisted briefly then turned away. Had he persisted, I'm not sure I would have won that fight, but I was prepared to give him some good whacks.

It never occurred to me that Mom may have actually wanted that man to come into the house; she was just too inebriated to respond to anything. Once I was certain he was gone, I got Mom into her bedroom, removed her contacts, and put her to bed. I have no idea if she remembered any of it.

Around this same time, my brother Scott was selling and using illegal drugs. When Mom was gone to the bars, he would host drug-infested parties at our house, often inviting 100 or more teenagers and young adults into our home. Alcohol and marijuana were the drugs of choice, budget or availability; but as the 1960's turned into the 1970's, harder drugs became available. I was 12, turning 13, now and trying to survive all that was happening from every angle of life.

One night at one Scott's parties, he was high on pot, and said that he and his friends would beat me up if I did not try it. Disgusted, I took a joint, made it look like I was inhaling the smoke, then I flipped the joint back at him and said, "There! Are you satisfied?" and walked away.

On another occasion, Scott had a pot party going on downstairs while my sisters had a drinking party going on upstairs. It was chaos. I was in my bedroom, trying to ignore it all and sleep. High or drunken couples kept trying to force their way into my bedroom so they could use my bed for their amorous intents, not knowing there was a kid (me) in there. So I lined up all my shoes, and when my door (which I could not lock) would open, I would throw a shoe at whoever was trying to come through as I yelled at them to get out.

That same night, Mom came home from a bar, and a State Patrol car pulled into the driveway behind her. Apparently he had just followed her because one of her tail-lights was out. He pulled up to our house, heard all the music, saw all the cars and all the people, and he knew there was trouble. One of Scott's friends, Tad, threw a beer bottle that shattered on the State Patrol officer's car, and … well, let's just say that chaos ensued.

The officer told Mom that he was leaving but would be back with more law enforcement in 10 minutes, to arrest anyone who was under-age while drinking. People started running every direction. I came out of my bedroom when I heard all the noise. As far as I was concerned, the officer could have taken all of them, right then.

Yet, I was invisible in this mess of kids. I found Mom outside and brought her back into the house, doing the usual drill of removing her contacts and getting her into her bed. Then I went back and started picking up thrown-away bottles and cans, and started cleaning up the house. I collected all of my shoes that were in the hall outside my bedroom door, and I finally put myself to bed. What else could go wrong?

Another Evil

Remember what I said earlier about Evil not stopping when a person is down? (This part is difficult to write about, so I'll preface it by saying in later years there was confession of wrongdoing, repentance and requesting forgiveness, and a degree of reconciliation; maybe not trust, but as least not residual unforgiveness and bitterness.) Read on ....

It was right around this same time that Scott began to sexually molest and physically abuse me. I was in early adolescence, and very vulnerable; I had a natural adolescent curiosity about sex. At first, there was a physical element of pleasure, but everything else about it was completely wrong. His abuse included various sexual activities that he either performed on me or made me do to him.

Sex has aspects of physical pleasure, yet it is so tied into our emotions — and when it is not by choice or happening with the wrong person, at the wrong time, under pressure — it messes people up big time. I was too young to know what to do, or if I should have resisted him more, if I could have resisted his greater physical strength at all.

With sexual abuse, part of you is excited about the arousal, yet part of you feels guilty that it is happening. My parents had not done a good job of either explaining, or modeling, what God plans for healthy sexuality within a committed marriage relationship. Teaching from the Catholic Church had not prepared me to deal with unwanted sexual advances. Sexual abuse distorts the boundaries which must be in place for normal humans, for our sexual and social development. Sexual abuse takes a thing — the God-ordained gift of sexual intimacy between a husband and a wife — and turns it into something damaged and broken, shattering the person as well as distorting the act.

For me, it was shattering. I knew I was in trouble, but I didn't want to be in trouble or get another person in trouble ... or have my Mom, who was already in her own set of troubles, become even more troubled by telling her what was happening. This abuse went on for several months.

Finally, I became big enough and learned I did have enough strength to stop him. Scott was doing more than sexually molesting me — he was also physically abusing me. Every time he would walk past, he would punch me; I would flinch every time he came by. On this day, he pinned me on the ground and forced our dog to attack me, biting me on my back. His game was for me to give in to him, or he would continue to have the dog attack me until I was bleeding. I was crying, yelling at him to get off of me; my back was bleeding, and it really hurt, but I would not say, *"Uncle"*!

Finally, seeing that my back was bleeding, Scott got off. I immediately jumped up and ran to our basement, where there was a bow and arrows on a rack. They were Sam's, which he used for hunting; powerful weapons, but I was now strong enough to use them. Scott saw me bring the bow and arrows, and knew exactly what I was planning — he ran into a bedroom and slammed the door, just as I shot the arrow, which pierced the wooden door about chest-level. Scott knew I was serious ... and he never touched me again.

I never told anyone about his abuse, nor my attempt to kill him that day.

Kids who are abused will either be self-destructive — which can play out with big problems or small problems, over time — or they will strike out at others — and sometimes, will be both self-destructive and will strike out at others. This evil can become their path in life. Until they experience love, grace and acceptance equal or greater than the damage they sustained.

It was only by the grace of God that I did not kill my brother. He stopped being my abuser, and, later in life, I forgave him. This happened because I realized that he too was a victim, and was passing forward the pain.

Several years ago, research was done leading to the development of objective criteria identifying experiences that — if or when occurring to children before the age of 18 — could contribute to the likelihood that those victims will have physical, emotional or other health challenges as adults. This research is known as **Adverse Childhood Experiences** (ACE) [5] . To assess this, a 10-question ACE survey was developed. If a person answers "Yes" to 4 or more of the 10 ACE survey questions, they are at greater risk. To put my childhood in perspective, my ACE score is 9 out of 10. Suffice it to say, my life would have taken a

---

[5] **Adverse childhood experiences** (ACEs) — a term coined by researchers Vincent Felitti, Robert Anda, and their colleagues in their seminal study conducted from 1995 to 1997 — are a subset of childhood adversities (April 10, 2019). Also see "Adverse childhood experiences are different than child trauma."

much different path without the involvement of caring adults, and the grace of God.

Personally, I am not a violent person. I was in rightful self-defense mode when I shot the arrow at Scott. I have never abused another in my life ... well, I guess I've been rough on the Football field, but that's legal and part of the game.

Physical and sexual abuse takes what is natural and even beautiful — a God-given capacity to love and be intimate with your spouse — and distorts it with guilt and confusion and shame. Often an abuser will threaten their victim, which breeds more fear and diminishment. Many times an abused person will struggle to know how to manage sex in their life, sometimes taking years to sort out. Sexual abuse can result in the victim seeking out more sexual experiences and stimulation, well before they are ready for a healthy relationship.

My own attraction to women was, in part, wholesome as women are beautiful; but I was also needing to confirm in myself that I was sexually normal in my own eyes. I wanted someone who made me feel valued and validated. This is true for most men, and likely women too. Having been abused impacted my ability to be emotionally intimate; it adversely impacted the development of my relationships.

All of this was a lot for a kid heading into middle school to process! I headed into my teenage years angry.

Chapter 7: **LIFE WITH DAD**

O ne day, **Mom set out on a two-week trip** with one of her boyfriends. She left a note for me saying she was leaving awhile, and she clipped a $20 bill on a memo board. It was a little trinket I had made at Scouts: a clothes-pin attached to a wooden dowel, with a wooden base. Mom's note said she would be gone about two weeks, and for me to use the money to buy food if I needed to.

Somehow the little hand-made memo board, with her note and the money, fell down, hiding in the space between the refrigerator and the kitchen countertop. I never saw it. I've sometimes wondered if this was an accident ... or could some Evil wind have tipped it over?

By this time, all my siblings were out of the house; it was just Mom and me, and now I was all alone. For the next two weeks I was responsible only for myself, and the safety of our house. Every morning, I would go to school, and every night, I would go to bed in the house alone, making sure to lock all the doors.

The food ran out pretty quickly — I was very thankful for school lunches, especially when I could go back for seconds. When I went to bed in the house alone, I admit I was scared, and yes, I prayed and would sometimes find sleep in those moments.

I was worried about where Mom had gone, but I didn't want to say anything to anybody at school for fear she would get into trouble, that her abandoning me alone would see me get put into foster care. I was losing her and what was left of my family.

Finally, Mom returned. She was very apologetic toward me, and vowed to never abandon me again. Yet, it wasn't long before she decided to leave Ephrata and move to Spokane. The pressure of her life, living in a small town, was just too much for her. Maybe she didn't want me to chase away any more of her boyfriends with my baseball bat!

She asked me if I wanted to move with her, or live with Dad. What a choice! By this time, I was in middle school, and did not want to leave my friends or quit my sports teams. I opted to live with Dad. I reasoned that I could live in my own bedroom, eat, sleep, and otherwise not engage with him or his new wife, yet still have access to my life, my friends, school and sports.

Mom moved to Spokane, and I moved in with Dad, still in Ephrata.

It worked pretty well at first; Dad and his new wife let me have my space. But something was happening in Dad's head, and he eventually decided he needed to establish himself in a stricter way in my life. He was over-compensating for having left the marriage and the family, and I was his target at hand to "make amends" over. He laid down strict rules, and he disregarded my wishes. This led to significant clashes between us. I gave him the nickname "Warden" when I spoke with my friends, although I did not share that with him.

"The Kindness of Strangers"

Our family loved to snow-ski, especially at Mission Ridge in Wenatchee. I started skiing when I was very young, and still have fond memories of those times. To help make money to buy my own ski-season tickets and even race on a Ski Team successfully, I had a route delivering newspapers. Skiing with the older kids and their friends pushed my skill development; it felt good to be good at something, and to have older kids recognize my abilities.

While I was living with Dad, one evening I was invited to a meeting at the home of one of my fellow Ski Team's parents. I walked into a living room full of parents from our town who all had kids who skied and raced. I did not realize that the meeting was for me, until I got there.

Ski racing is expensive, and to really compete, you need different types of skis for different events; it also requires financial support to attend races, pay entry fees, etc. This group of parents was offering to pay for my equipment and costs to keep racing. I was beyond words — thankful, for sure, but also embarrassed that this was coming from people other than my family. They knew my parents could not — or would not — afford to support my ski racing.

Politely, I thanked them for their offer, but never responded to it either. After that, I raced a bit more but was not comfortable taking money or support from others, and a newspaper route did not provide enough funding to keep it going. When my equipment failed or needed replacement. I could not keep up with the costs. My racing transitioned into recreational skiing; I did not pursue competitive skiing.

This was happening during the transition from living with Mom and then moving in with Dad; between my 7th and 8th grades. I did not have the insights, emotional intelligence, or perspective to understand the significance of these events at that time in my life. I share this to show that the love and grace of strangers is a powerful thing in a person's life. Even though I did not accept their offer, just the fact that it was made validated something about me, enriched a place inside me that helped me value myself more.

> *"Schedule kindness in your day. Watch how small acts of kindness can change your mood, bring someone else joy, and give both of you a positive benefit."*
> — **Germany Kent**

> *"Kindness is the language which the deaf can hear and the blind can see."*
> — **Anonymous**

The Value of Sports

Another thing: looking back at this from the lens of my career in public education, it also shows how financial barriers cause opportunity gaps which are usually the cause of the performance gaps that we spend so much time being concerned about in our culture! Society invests a lot of time and energy perseverating over the movements of the windmill blades, but fails to understand or effectively address the winds that cause them to move.

I know there are many different opinions about Sports. My purpose is not to entertain or further debate this now; however, suffice it to say that me playing Sports while growing up was life-saving. I learned so many life skills from coaches, team-mates, the games, practicing, self-discipline, setting and working toward goals, and more. I could even take out my frustration in an organized manner! While I enjoyed many activities, Football was the most direct way to express myself. It was in my life, the only sane and rational way for me to express myself.

It was easy for me to stay away from alcohol or drugs because I saw the damage it did to my family. God lead me away from those things. I really poured myself into playing Football, likely making it my "god" for many years, through high school. I think God knew I needed Football too, perhaps even let me lean on it awhile, until He wanted me to set it down and pick up leaning on Him more. I suspect we all use crutches to walk when we otherwise would limp, until God heals those tender places in our hearts and we learn to lean on Him and walk with Him more exclusively along Life's path.

Just as forces of Evil reach into our lives to rape our hearts, God uses people to reaching into our lives to rescue our hearts. Love heals! In this respect, life is a bit of a playground where we are each given freedom of choice of the many options in the game — except Life is not a game and is far from a playground. Life is very real. God knows that, and sometimes we can become aware that God is involved in our lives, sometimes not.

I am not exactly sure where some of my public school teachers and coaches were in their own faith, but I know that three or four of them were used to intercept, support, confront, and show love to me in those "middle" years. Their advice and care for me, the direction they provided, gave me the words of a father in a real, tangible way that I needed, helping me sort my way through school and through life. Sometimes this would be a teacher or a coach pulling me aside and talking with me about what was happening at school, in sports or in my life, but it made a difference.

By today's criteria, my "group" back then socially would be called a "gang." These were kids from broken or dysfunctional homes; most were using drugs of some sort; some wore the "outcast culture" related clothes. They were often in trouble at school; having collisions with authorities; some being beaten by parents. Most were sexually active, with girls who had similar stories. Some were siblings of actual gang members, who had their own scars. I hung out with them, but wasn't active like they were.

Despite all these negatives, we were an amazingly accepting group, and nobody judged anyone else as long as you were in the gang. We were sort of like an "island of unconditional acceptance," but also a mix of lifestyles that were dangerous on many levels. I was the non-drinker who did not do drugs; nobody pressured me, although they would always offer, and usually talked about how good it made them feel. I saw what drinking and drugs had done to my family, and was never tempted to do alcohol or drugs — it was an easy "No" for me.

During all this mess, I was still feeling God's presence in me, although I sometimes could not put a name to it. I was rarely frightened by anything external; I knew what was okay or not okay for me. I added value to our "gang" because I was so good at Sports — one of the few 7th graders who was allowed to play in a 9th grade Football game, which almost never happened in those days. I gained so many yards rushing in my first 7th grade Football game that they stopped recording them early in the second half, when I got over 250 yards.

This success also gave me recognition with the "good kids" at school, but I liked the guys in my "gang" because they were real to me, I felt more understood and accepted in their circle than with the kids who did not have the family scars which the rest of us carried — at least, at that time I did not know how many of the "good kids" had to deal with things in their families too. I learned that later.

The group that I ran with was actually very dangerous; later in life, some were killed in drug-related incidents, or car accidents, or other tragedies. I had left this group long before that happened, but only because of one coach.

Chapter 8: **CHANGING THE TRAJECTORY**

L **eaving that gang was because** of a teacher and coach named Marty O'Brien. He was the Physical Education teacher at my middle school. One day after class, he called me into his office, and said, "Nick, I understand that you have been going through things at home that nobody should have to experience. I am sorry this has happened to you." As I listened, I wondered to what extent he really knew what I was going through, how did he know anything about me? Now, I think that Mom was "behind that curtain," and had shared some things with him.

He continued to share how he saw something special in me. He was concerned that the gang I was running with was not going to end up well; if I stayed with that group, it could really hurt me later. Marty O'Brien knew I wanted to pursue Football, and he used that to help me identify with my life goals at that time.

I spent some energy defending "my guys," sharing why I did not like the "plastic simplicity" of the "good kids." He replied that some of them had more challenges than I realized. He asked me to consider making different friends. That was the talk.

A few days later, what he had said was resonating in that place in my heart — the same place where God resides — and I knew I needed to act on it. I have learned that when God wants me to make a change or act in some direction, He can be very persistent!

In the school hallway a few days later, I spoke with Casey, the leader of our gang, and told him I was going to stop hanging out with them. I told him why too. Casey became angry, pulled a knife on me and said I could not leave.

It would have been a hard fight, because he was tough, but I replied that if I had to fight him so I could leave, I would. He cussed at me ... and walked away. Some time later, another guy from the gang faced off with me in the hallway; we did a little pushing and shoving into the lockers, but that was quickly stopped by a teacher, who sent us both to the principal's office. That was the end of my time in that gang.

This changed the trajectory of my life. I did make friends with some of the "good" kids. Most of the guys who stayed in that gang were killed, dropped out of school, or died early as adults from medically-related consequences of their lifestyle choices. If I would have stayed in that gang, I don't think I could have avoided what caught up with them in later life. I was just keeping my own head above water, and benefitting from being away from their activities, many of which were dangerous.

Sometimes a teacher or coach would show particular interest in me and make me feel valued. I remember Mr. Archer in 8th grade, commenting on one of my assignments in his class, and feeling valued for something I did that was not on the Football field. That felt pretty good too.

Another teacher who was also a coach, Mr. McMillian, told me he named his third son after me and hoped he would grow up to be like me! I was humbled and overwhelmed, feeling that I should have told him how messed up inside I was; I thought he should change the name before it was too late, to not put that pressure on his kid. But I did not want to share my truths with him either. While it felt good to experience such praise, I also remember not feeling worthy. Deep inside, I still carried shame and embarrassment from the rough life I had experienced.

Transformational Love

In the spring of my Junior year in high school, I decided to not play Baseball; instead, I chose to run Track, mostly to help develop my speed for Football. After I left the Baseball team, Dave Johnson — a Hall of Fame Baseball coach — continued to reach out to me, respecting my choice. He also helped me deal with some challenges I was having at home. Once he gave me a ride to Spokane to see my mother — and I wasn't even on his Baseball team anymore! In him, and these other influences, I met God — that is, **"God as my Father" was modeled through these coaches and teachers.** Yes, this was happening in public schools!

This was a big deal for me, especially with Dave Johnson, because he was showing love for me even when I was not an athlete contributing to his Sport or his team. Somehow, when a person treats well another who can do nothing for them in return — this has always been for me the most powerful form of showing God's love in this world. That kind of unselfish love transforms people. So often we see "love" passed around as a trade, a form of "transactional love" where one loves in exchange or on the condition of getting something back from the other person. That's not God's kind of love.

God demonstrates His own love for us in this: while we were still sinners, Christ died for us.

Romans 5:8

I will share more about these "angels" in my life, and introduce you to a few others, a bit later in this book. Thankfully, God's greatest gift of His Son, Jesus, was a transformational gift because there sure wasn't anything anybody — not the people who were alive back then, nor anyone alive today — could ever do to earn that type of love.

We will never "deserve" God's love — He offers it without conditions

If I sent my son to save the lives of people, and then they lied about him and chased him and finally killed him, treating Jesus the way they did, I am pretty sure I would not respond with love and forgiveness in the light of salvation.

The influence and impact of these public school teachers and coaches was so significant that, when I was in my early 20s in college, trying to decide on my major and career of choice, I decided to go into Education, to become a teacher and a coach. I have been a public school educator for over 32 years, a superintendent for 22 of those years. Really, I am still that teacher and coach, just in a bigger "classroom."

When I made that career choice, I wanted to do something that mattered — just as these people had mattered to me while I was growing up. That decision was, quite simply, to devote my life and any God-given talents, to make a positive difference in the lives of others. Just as some had done for me, I wanted to do for others. When, as a new teacher and coach, I got my first briefcase, I set the combination to "113" in honor of "1st Corinthians 13," often called "the Love Chapter." The importance of keeping love as the center of our being and actions, is critically important. I wanted to be that type of Educator. I will share more about these public school experiences later in this book.

*If I speak in the languages of men or of angels —
but do not have love — I am only a resounding
gong or a clanging cymbal. If I have the gift of
prophecy and can fathom all mysteries and all
knowledge, and if I have faith that can move
mountains — but do not have love — I am
nothing. If I give all I possess to the poor and
give over my body to hardship that I may boast
— but do not have love — I gain nothing.*

*Love is patient, love is kind. It does not envy, it
does not boast, it is not proud. It does not
dishonor others, it is not self-seeking, it is not
easily angered, it keeps no record of wrong.
Love does not delight in evil but rejoices with
the truth. It always protects, always trusts,
always hopes, always perseveres.*

*Love never fails. But where there are
prophecies, they will cease; where there are
languages, they will be stilled, where there is
knowledge, it will pass away. For we know in
part and we prophecy in part, but when
completeness comes, what is in part disappears.
When I was a child, I talked like a child, I
thought like a child, I reasoned like a child.*

When I became a man, I put the ways of childhood behind me. For now we see only a reflection as in a mirror; then we shall see face to face. Now I know in part; then I shall know fully, even as I am fully known.

And now these three remain: faith, hope and love. But the greatest of these is love.

1st Corinthians 13:1-13

Chapter 9: **THE HOLY SPIRIT, TEACHER**

The Bible is filled with such wonderful knowledge!

"If you love Me, keep My commands. And I will ask the Father, and He will give you another Advocate to help you and be with you forever — the Spirit of Truth. The world cannot accept Him because it neither sees Him nor knows Him. But you know Him for He lives with you and will be in you.

"I will not leave you as orphans; I will come to you. Before long, the world will not see Me anymore, but you will see Me. Because I live, you also will live. On that day, you will realize that I am in My Father, and you are in Me and I am in you. Whoever has My commands and keeps them is the one who loves Me. The one who loves Me will be loved by My Father, and I will will love them and show Myself to them."

John 14:15-21

Living with Dad was just odd — there is not another word for it. Dad did not "walk his talk." He would say things, but then not live or act consistently with what he said he believed. I am sure this is true, to some extent, for many of us, from time to time. For most Christians, it is a daily process of *"working out our salvation"* (see Philippians 2:12-13). But I just did not see the "fruit" in my Dad's life. There seemed to be a profound disconnect that happened all the time. One of my friends even commented to me about him in this way, and said his parents would have adopted me as their son because I did not deserve much of the stuff I put up with from Dad.

Dad was pursuing a series of "religious activities," but not starting with the most basic step: of asking God to come inside and clean out his heart. [6] Dad was following some kind of "self-help," "modernization" project of himself, and he was not able to hear and follow God's lead from the inside out. I never figured that out.

I was busy with school and sports, and had even joined some Youth and Bible Study groups. These were good places to learn more about the teachings in the Bible and explore different concepts of being a Christian. Some of the group leaders were good people, would spend time talking with me and answering questions about God since I was curious to know more about Him.

One man in particular, Glen, led a Youth Group in which I participated with a number of my teenaged peers. In addition to learning about the Bible, Glen would help us talk about things that were happening in our lives. For his regular job, Glen worked as a Probation Officer.

One day, Glen invited me to ride along on a visit to a family that was assigned to him. We drove from Ephrata to some rural property just outside of Moses Lake, about 20 miles away. As we traveled, the paved road turned to gravel, then the gravel ran thin, and the last quarter-mile was dirt.

---

[6] See 1st John 1:9

When we arrived, Glen said it would be best for me to wait in the car as he went to the house to check if everything was okay. I watched as a girl a bit younger than me greeted Glen at the door. They spoke for awhile, then he motioned for me to come and join him. I did not say much to anyone as he talked with the family.

There were three girls; the oldest was about 12, next about 10, and the youngest about 8 years old. The dirt from the front yard was caked on the concrete steps and running in through the front door. Actually, there was no front door. Dirt continued into the entry of the house, which had carpet worn bare in a fan-shaped pattern, to the wooden floor. I could see a mix of human garbage and dog feces, inside the house and outside in the yard.

The three kids were dressed, but did not look like they had bathed for some time. Glen asked if they had been eating; the older girl said, "Yes, I am looking out for them." We continued into the kitchen, and the only food anywhere was about one-third of a 5-pound bag of white sugar; this was open on the counter. This is what they had been eating.

Glen asked where their mother was, and she said she had been gone about three days. The older girl was left to get the younger ones to school, but had been struggling with this — this is why Glen was given the task to check on the family. There were no parents or other adults at the house.

Glen talked a bit longer with the oldest girl, then said it was time for us to go. On the way back, he shared that he would need to call another department to rescue the kids from that derelict situation, then make another to follow-up with the mother, who clearly was not able to be responsible for them. He did not know if the foster system would be able to keep all of them together; chances were high that the sisters would be separated.

As an educator, I have often thought about that visit, about the challenges in life and learning that result from this kind of situation for kids; and how schools seek to educate and support and address such profound needs. As we drove back to Ephrata that day, I also though that while my childhood had been challenging, there were some kids who had it even tougher than me.

I don't know if it was Glen's purpose for taking me on that trip, but it sure seemed like God used it to teach me that, no matter how bad I may think my life is at any time, there are always those who have it worse. Maybe this was the start of the road of learning on how to be content with God in any situation, even when the road gets bumpy. [7]

In the few years that I lived with Dad and his second wife Sue, I could never establish a good relationship with her; I think she just tolerated my presence in "her house." At least, that's what I felt. I don't think I made much effort with her either. I kept to myself, and we managed okay. Sometimes I would go to Spokane to visit Mom during the summer; life seemed to be settling down.

---

[7] See Philippians 4:11-13

Divine Encounter

I clearly recall one day learning about *"the gift of being filled with the Holy Spirit."* [8]

I had read about this in the Bible, and accepted it as truth. I sincerely believed the Bible is the inspired Word of God, not fiction. I began to want to "experience the Holy Spirit" myself. I went into my room, closed the door, sat down on my bed and prayed, with that same honest and child-like faith and clarity of motive and heart. As I prayed, I felt a tightening in my chest; I wondered if I was having heart attack. Then a rush that felt like wind filled my chest, but it was not from taking a breath. I was light-headed, but not at all alarmed or concerned; actually, I felt an indescribable peace.

I don't remember falling off the bed, but I ended up on the floor. I had this really clear image of laying at the feet of Jesus. I was also given a small phrase to pray in a language I did not understand. That was the beginning of "the gift of speaking in tongues."

Over the years, that small phrase grew and grew into a full language; it's called *"a Heavenly language."* I have prayed with that, mostly secretly, for years; it is like the most direct connection I can access when I need to fuel up my heart. I don't speak in my Heavenly language around other people. I pray in English so it doesn't weird-out people who don't understand "the gift of the Holy Spirit" which includes "a Heavenly

---

[8] Also see Acts 2:1-8, 11-12, 14-21; Isaiah 59:21; Luke 11:13; John 14:16; Acts 2:38-39, 10:44-45.

language." This is my truth to share; deal with it however you can.

That image of me laying at the feet of Jesus is also often one I go back to in prayer, especially when I have really made a mess of things, especially when I have tried to do my own thing in life without following God's leading. All to often we rush head-long and head-strong into doing things in our lives, then find ourselves praying for help when it all hits the fan and we are in trouble. Most often now, I will pray before setting about things, which seems to create the right order of importance or priority, and then the day or events open up in a better way.

Still, when I am quietly praying, or when I'm listening for God's lead or direction about something, I frequently relate to that place in me when I first truly encountered that humble place of "being with Jesus," even if I was laying flat at His feet. It is both a physical sense or image, and a spiritual place of awareness, of oneness and connecting with God. I go in to His presence with a question, and come out with some insight, or words, or direction. He doesn't fail me, ever.

It is sort of like a "Heavenly version of GPS" (which I mentioned earlier), where we can tune into that leading and follow it. When we don't tune in, we can make choices on our own, which often take us off course. Using our free and independent will is a crap-shoot and often confusing — connecting with God and His guidance brings peace and confidence.

After making poor choices, ending up off-road, we can always go back so that *"still, small Voice"* (see 1st Kings 19:12) within us can speak and show us how to get back on track. God forgives us like that! We can accept this forgiveness, and forgive ourselves, and get back on track at any time. Or we can be stubborn, beat our heads and hearts against the walls we have created … and then blame God for it.

That's one of the loudest criticisms of Christianity: *"How can a loving God let so much wickedness win, so many bad things happen?"* That's basically "passing the buck" — refusing to take responsibility for our own actions, and trying to find someone else to blame. This behavior has been around since the Garden of Eden, when Adam tried to blame Eve for all the sin that had come into the world. [9]

Nobody told Adam he had to eat it, that was his choice. God laid down the tules, and the pair of them (with help from Satan) broke them. God's tules are still there, but it seems like one of humanity's favorite occupations is tule-breaking, and then blaming God because of the mess we make. Adam and Eve (and all of humanity) had a long way to go.

Many times too, when we get off track, when we realize the errors (or sins) of our own making, we can get very down on ourselves and begin to feel ourselves unworthy of a relationship with God. We count ourselves out of the plan, we disconnect from the relationship. **What we really need to do is to accept our fallibility as part of the human condition, and ask God for His continued grace and intervention in our lives, to try to keep moving forward with God.** Evil does try to throw us off track from the life we have with

9 See Genesis 3:11-12

God, that's true — but sometimes we disqualify ourselves too. It all comes down to choice.

Chapter 10: **DECLARING INDEPENDENCE**

Dad's second marriage did end in divorce. I don't remember much about it; I think he told me rather off-handedly as we were driving somewhere. I don't recall having any emotion one way or the other about that news. The best outcome of that marriage was a son they had, who has become really a neat young man. John is now grown and married, with his own children, and is a good person. I only spent a little time with him when he was young, before I moved away.

While I was in high school, Dad and I moved into another house in Ephrata. It wasn't long before Dad was dating again, and then married a woman named Shirley. This was the person with whom he spent the rest of his life. I liked Shirley; the only thing I did not understand about her was why in the world she would hook up with my Dad! For some reason, she loved him; possibly because he had learned enough over his life how to treat a wife appropriately.

There were still big gaps in what he would preach and how he would actually live. By this time, I was nearly ready to leave home; I was staying with Dad and Shirley just long enough to graduate from high school and then move out.

At Dad's house, my bedroom was on the front side of the house; Dad's was on the back. There was also an old cement swimming pool in the backyard. One night, I heard the faint sound of a cat crying, but it seemed far away. It was not uncommon for neighborhood cats to get into fights, as folks let them run loose outside, especially at night. The next morning, I was standing in the kitchen fixing myself breakfast, looking out a back window, when I noticed something floating in the swimming pool. It was a dead cat. I exclaimed, "Dad, do you see that?"

"Yes," he answered. "I heard it crying all night. It was stuck in the pool and could not get out."

Dumbfounded, I asked, "If you heard it crying, knowing it was not able to get out, why wouldn't you get up and scoop it out with the pool skimmer?"

He replied, "Well, I thought by leaving it in the pool, that would teach the cat a lesson." I did not know what to think. Part of me wanted to scream, but I just swallowed and left the room.

Dad let me sleep in a room in his house without paying rent. He prepared one meal each day — for which he was quite proud of himself — and then I had to fend for myself for the rest of the meals. He let me use his truck now and then, to see my friends, provided I put my own gas in, earned from my part-time jobs, and did plenty of chores around the house. Dad did not interfere with my sports; other than acting as my "warden" to restrict my comings and goings, we simply coexisted in his house.

The "warden" thing may seem like any typical teenager's resistance to normal parental supervision — and yes, I do believe teenagers need parental supervision. However, at 12 years old, I had been supervising my drunken Mom, taking care of the house, working a newspaper route and another weekend job at a local veterinarian's clinic, surviving being abused by my brother, and dealing with all the craziness of other events in my life. I was responsible because I had to be — nobody else was responsible.

When Dad tried to shift me back into this "parental supervision of teenager mode" without understanding or acknowledging how responsible and mature I had already become by then, I was hurt and angry. He did not really know me, did not know anything about my reality, and frankly, he didn't realize the growing-up I had to do on my own as a result of **his** poor life choices. I did not have the verbal skills or emotional comprehension to actually process this with Dad at the time. I don't think he was equipped to process it with me either. He didn't know me.

Later, when I was leaving for college, I received from him a graduation gift: luggage. Paper-thin, inexpensive luggage that nested all the pieces together so I could slide it all under the bed for storage. Cheap luggage or not, it was both functional and symbolic: after using it, I never spent another night under his roof after I left for college.

Later in life, my wife thought we should go visit Dad, so that our kids could know him and perhaps develop a normal relationship with their grandfather. I tried to explain I didn't think it was a good idea, but — like the Santa Claus myth — there were some things just not worth fighting over. So we went to visit him ... and as we were driving home, she said, of her own choice, "We don't have to go back. It's fine if the kids don't get to know him." I started laughing so hard that I had to pull over the car so I wouldn't lose control of the vehicle.

The Lamp Story

There's one more "Dad story" to share, mostly for its comedy relief. It was a capstone moment, and reflected well what our relationship — or rather, lack of relationship — was about.

It was June of my senior year in high school. I had earned all kinds of recognition for my success with Football; I was headed to a major university on a full scholarship. Although I went to high school mainly for Sports and to date girls, and I enjoyed hobbies with cars and motorcycles, I had also managed to keep a 3.4-GPA (B+) in my scholastic work without ever taking books home to study. I don't recommend that approach to Academics, and certainly have expected more from the children whom I taught as students.

There was not much positive or Academic role-modeling happening in my life in those days. I planned to go to college to play Football ... or if I didn't, then I was going to ride a motorcycle across country until I ran out of money. Then I would find some kind of job and work, and make enough money to ride further. I didn't have any plan beyond that.

I'm not proud of that now, but I want to be truthful. I didn't really like the academic part of school. I know now that I could have done so much better academically in school, but I was so bored with most of my classes and had little, if any, interest in the assigned subjects. Only on one occasion did a teacher make something interesting and relevant to the class; otherwise, school was really just access to Sports and all the other interests I had then.

I was the kid nobody wanted to invite to their parties — but not because I was unpopular — because I was self-imposed, super-strict about not drinking beer or anything alcoholic, about not smoking pot, about not doing anything harmful to my body. Had Dad known this, he would have had reason to be proud of what I had accomplished. As I was nearing "leaving the nest," he could have recognized these things ... but he didn't.

On the night of graduation from high school, when almost everyone I knew — all my friends and classmates — were at parties. Being the self-appointed "designated sober for life" person I had always been — and knowing that I made my peers uncomfortable if I attended their parties — it was different for me. I invited Lorraine, a girl from my class, to just hang out with me. We were not making out — we were simply sitting in the living room at my Dad's house on the night of graduation, just visiting. Why Lorraine agreed to eschew all the other parties still escapes me.

In Dad's living room, there were lamps where the bases had lights in them, as well as three-way bulbs at the top. Lorraine and I were sitting in the living room, talking, when Dad walks into the room and turns all the bulbs of both lamps onto the highest setting. It was almost bright enough to get suntanned! Dad then looked at us and said, *"Evil lurks in the dark!"* and walked out of the room.

I was embarrassed. Lorraine was embarrassed. Knowing all the unsafe things we could have been doing that night, but instead were calmly sitting in plain sight, just visiting ... and then he pulls this out of his religious nut hat. We left, just drove around. We did not go drinking. We did not have sex. We talked about life, about God, about what would happen after we left home. And we avoided talking about my crazy, judgmental father.

With all the bravado and emotions of graduation, it can be a really scary time for most young adults. The most frequently asked question: *"What are you going to do after high school?"* You develop a plan so you can share something; that seems to be okay for most people who ask — but the truth is: you really don't know if that plan will work, or if you will even want to continue that plan after you start it. Still, you feel like you're supposed to have it all figured out.

Also, you know you need to leave, but you're not sure if you are ready, or exactly if you have what you need to deal with the known and unknown challenges coming next. It's not an easy time at all.

Leaving Dad

The "lamp story" has an exciting finish, so stay with me. It was now August that same summer after graduation, and Dad was in the living room with his soon-to-be third wife (remember I said, Shirley is a nice person). It was beginning to be dusk outside, not dark night but certainly the sun was dimming. I walked into the living room and found them there — and of course I turned both of those lamps to full strength! I looked right at Dad and quoted, *"Evil lurks in the dark!"*

Do you remember those cartoons where the comic character turns angry, his face goes red and steam blows out of his ears? That was Dad — except now I was six-feet tall and 190 pounds of lean mass, who could bench-press 325 pounds and squat over 550 pounds by then. I had been doing my summer workout prior to reporting for college and Football. The percentage of my body fat was so low that, even with a full breath of air, I could not float in a swimming pool.

Off the football field, I was a nice, calm, flannel-shirted, sweet-tempered person. There had been only two fights in school (the one I mentioned earlier when, in middle school, I left the "gang"; and another one in high school when I defended a special-education student who was being harassed and bullied by another kid; I'll tell this story later). On this day, in that moment, I was done with my father. I was not *"turning the other cheek,"* I was not taking his wrath anymore. I didn't scream. I didn't swallow. I didn't back down. I was simply done with him.

I was leaving the house with a set of cheap new luggage (at least I said, "Thank you"), heading to college without needing one penny of support from him. I was finished with his crap and was not going to take it anymore. The whole *"honor thy parents"*[10] and *"turn the other cheek"*[11] things just didn't apply for me right then — I think God laughed at that one too ... or maybe He cheered for me, knowing we would deal with those attitudes later. It was what it was.

Several weeks before, I had declared my independence: **my Dad was not in my life anymore. I had divorced him.** I left the house and got a ride to college with someone other than my Dad. He wasn't

---

[10] See Ephesians 6:2

[11] See Matthew 5:39

there for me when I needed him, he wasn't there for me in the ways that I needed him, so I chose to not need him either, Ever. That is what I learned from my Earthly father. I thank God that He is my Heavenly Father, and that He brought many other good men and women who came alongside me on Life's path.

Even after this break with Dad, I continued seeking others whom I had adopted throughout my life, for wisdom, guidance or advice — I needed these people in my life. God continued to use these people, even bringing new people into my path, most often exactly the time when I needed them.

It would be almost 30 years later when Dad and I would talk on the phone. My sisters had urged me to speak with him sooner, but I was not ready. Finally, we did have several phone conversations. He tearfully apologized for his failures being a father to me. He acknowledged that he had not been there for me; he explained he thought he was doing the best he could but that it was not very good at all. Now Dad shared how proud he was of me, but also how embarrassing it would be when people would share how good I was in Sports, mostly Football — but he knew next to nothing about it. He said he felt totally inept as my father.

I forgave him. I told him he did not need to feel badly. I shared that my life had turned out okay — because I had been fathered by God. Either directly or indirectly, God had seen to my fathering through the lives of other people who stepped in to fill the missing parts. I told Dad to be at peace, to enjoy the remainder of his life.

He thanked me; by the end of those few phone calls, I could hear a different tone in his voice. After Dad passed, Shirley told me those calls made a difference in him. I don't know for sure how much those calls mattered to me. It seemed like he had died to me so many years before that when his body finally died, it was a bit anti-climatic in my world.

A Handrail On the Stairs in the Dark

Look: nobody is a perfect parent, and there are no perfect children. If you are a parent, do a good job with your children. If you mess up, admit it, try to fix it, keep at it. If your kids mess up, teach them to admit it and to fix it. Most importantly, get yourself connected to God — and your kids connected to God — so He can be openly, actively helping you along Life's path. God is faithful, and He will be with your kids in your absence.

What we say to our children is important — it shows what we believe — and then what we model to our kids will mean even more. You can be a friend but not their buddy. They will need you differently depending on their age, so be ready to change how you parent them as the road grows longer and they get older. You will always be their parent. They may think they are okay without you, but they will be better if you are healthy and available for them.

I have two very capable young adult kids and two amazing teen stepsons who still, on occasion, reach out to me — much like the person who seeks the handrail when going up a flight of stairs in the dark. Be there for your kids as they do need you. Love them as God loves us!

Chapter 11: *"IN THE COMPANY OF ANGELS"* [12]

There were several inches of fresh snow fallen
over the existing snow. Snowplows had piled up
what was scraped off the main streets, into rows
along each side limiting the space between the parked
cars and the lanes of traffic. It was just turning evening;
with the winter daylight hours, it was already very dark.
It was quiet and sound muted with the snow absorbing
so much of the noise of cars and town. There were still
flakes falling but they were in no hurry as they floated
down, highlighted by street lights as though each one
was on its own special showcase journey to the Earth.

It was my junior year in high school, and I was
working at a part-time after-school job at a local glass
store. They made picture frames, replaced broken glass
in house windows, and replaced windshields in cars.
My job was mostly cleaning up the place after the day's
business, and occasionally I helped the guy who
replaced car windshields.

Near the end of a shift, they asked me to drive a
customer's car from the backside of the shop around to
park it on the street in front of the store; we had just
replace the windshield. The customer would be in later
to pick it up. So I drove the car around and parked in
the space right in front of the store.

Then, because of my age, I started to do what I often
did: I placed one hand on the car's door and the other
on the seat, intending to enable myself to vault out of

---

12 See Hebrews 13:2

the car and land on my feet outside, even shutting the car door, all in one move. Don't ask me to do that now — I was a kid, and it was an athletic move. I liked to do it for fun.

This time was different. I parked the car, turned off the motor, placed the car-key above the visor for the customer to retrieve, pulled on the door handle, placed my hands in position, and was about to launch myself out the car door into the street … when I heard an audible Voice say, *"STOP!"*

Immediately the hair on the back of my neck stood up. I thought, *"Uh oh, someone is in the car!"* So I turned around to check the back-seat — it was empty. I checked the radio — it was off. Then I turned to look at the partially open door, awaiting my flashy vaulting exit — and a very large Public Utility District truck was passing the car at that very moment. It was massive, it was heavy, and — in the snow-covered streets — was nearly silent. It was so close to the car that the wind of the truck's passing was pulling so much on the door that I had to hold it firmly to keep it from being opened wider.

If I had not stopped when I heard that Voice, I would have jumped right out of the car into the oncoming truck, with no way of escape being smashed!

Okay, some of you are thinking, *"Nick, you must have imagined hearing that Voice. Or maybe some other instinctive thought caused you to check for traffic before you got out of the car."* **Not the case.** I was launching myself out of the car when I heard the audible Voice warning, *"STOP!"* This was not a *"burning bush"* [13] and there was no other sound. I was alone in the car … I thought.

I sat back in the car and processed it. I don't know if I heard the voice of God, or if it was a Voice of an angel sent from God, but for certain, that Voice made sure I did not die that day. I don't need you to believe me — I was there, and I know it happened.

I returned to the store, still processing what had just happened. My understanding of these things does not depend on you. I share this event as an example of where there is "an intervention" in our lives. They are usually just in time and, often in a way to help us accomplish something relevant or necessary for us.

God Gets Involved In Our Lives

At times, God's interventions in our lives will be rather direct; at other times, He will come through the actions or words of others. Allow me to share a few which were both simple and profound; you can make of them what you want. When these things have happened, I always remember the details.

Once I was sitting in fourth-period Chemistry class, which was right after lunch. I was talking with Johnathan, a foreign-exchange student from New Zealand, asking him to help me understand the concept of a *"mole."* Not the furry creature that digs tunnels in our yards, or a dark mark on our skin — a "mole" is a unit of measurement in Science. The teacher, Leo McIntee, was preparing to show us a

---

[13] See Exodus 3.

movie — wait! *"A movie in Chemistry?"* I thought. *"How exciting!"*

A quick segue (because I like to recognize teachers): Leo McIntee was a great teacher, full of school spirit. He would even lead the cheering section during Football games by going out in front of the students and parents and getting everyone pepped up. He was a great role model.

Back to the story. The movie was started and had been playing about 10 minutes when Bobby, a student near the front of the class, stood up and rushed toward the sink on the other side of the laboratory room. Bobby was literally throwing up his lunch as he ran. The spray of vomit arced across the projection of the movie, creating a grisly shade on the screen; it looked almost like something from an old horror movie.

Immediately, everyone in the class grabbed their own stomachs, or clamped their hands across their own mouths, and groaned. Bobby — the student who was unfortunately seeing his lunch again from a whole new perspective as it splashed into the sink — was mortified. The movie stopped and the lights went on.

The entire class was in a state of shock, which quickly morphed into derision and rudeness. Poor Bobby was still at the sink in front of the room, having dry heaves, which can produce a sound greater than the outcome, but the pain is worse.

The whole class awaited Mr. McIntee's response. Once pale-faced Bobby was now turning red, partly from the vomiting but also from the embarrassment of doing it in front of the whole class — and onto the movie screen, no less! In a very loving and apologetic way, Mr. McIntee said aloud so the whole class could hear, "Bobby, I am so sorry; I did not think the movie was that bad."

The class roared in laughter. 100% of their laughter was directed at Mr. McIntee's comment, not at Bobby. The teacher moved to Bobby's side, put his arm around him until he had stopped vomiting, then had a couple of students help him down to the School Nurse's office.

When Bobby was out of the classroom, Mr. McIntee talked with us about how embarrassing this had been for Bobby, and asked us to keep that in mind in the days that followed. To my knowledge, nobody ever teased Bobby about that; most just checked to see he was doing okay, or thanked him for breaking up the movie and making Science class more interesting.

It is my belief that Leo McIntee was a Christian; I know his daughter was, and I believe that Christianity had become a family thing. In my estimation, Leo McIntee was acting as an angel for Bobby that day, and a teacher for all of us well beyond Chemistry.

I was learning kindness and sympathy.

Teachers Who Cared

The next year, my junior year, I was in Literature class. This class was mostly reading "great works of literature" and then writing a report or discussing them in class. Some books were interesting to me; some were more "words of endurance." Our teacher, Mabel Thompson, was an older woman who was very energetic. Often when we were sharing in class, she would rise up on her toes and say, *"Be specific!"* any time we referenced some part of a novel. She was thin, slightly built, but could command respect from everyone for the way she interacted with people. She put up her hair in a tight bun, and wore dramatic long dresses, and had eyes that could nearly look right through you.

On this particular day I recall, the whole class was reading quietly. Mrs. Thompson was not a coach of mine; I really didn't know her beyond this class. As far as I knew, I was just another student in her class. Sometimes teachers and students have a stronger connection, perhaps even the student works as a teacher's assistant. This was not the case with Mrs. Thompson and me.

So there I was, reading *"Les Misérables,"* and actually getting into the story. Mrs. Thompson stood next to my desk. I stop reading because she was just standing there; I looked up at her. She said, ***"You need to do something important with your life."***

Being a typical high school male, I did not understand her meaning. I said, "Huh?"

She repeated the statement, "You need to do something important with your life."

I said, "Okay" — but really don't comprehend what she was saying to me, at age 17. She never explained what she meant. Only years afterward, that phrase would come back to me, over and over.

For instance, I would be at a crossroad in life, doing something that might lead to a career or lead down another path, and Mrs. Thompson's comment would resound. I often asked myself, "What is that 'important thing' I'm supposed to be doing? Is this it, or not?" I began to feel that God was speaking directly to me, and that sometimes He spoke to me through others.

I don't know if Mabel Thompson was a Christian, but she was an angel to me; her message resonated for many years after that class. I can barely remember the books we read, or even what I learned from them; I can't recall one single assignment from that class either. But my whole life, I have remembered her comment. To this day, I have no idea what inspired or motivated her to say it — still, God used her that day in my life.

I was learning to listen to God's leading.

Being God's Instrument

David was a Special Education student who was being mainstreamed in our Physical Education class. He lived in a foster home; he wore large black-framed glasses. The glasses were so broken and taped, and the lenses so thick, that if you walked near him and the sunlight hit them just right, it would actually throw a light-prism on the ground.

David was socially awkward and very needy; he would bug the other kids to get their attention; at times, the attention he got was not appropriate. David was not cool. He was not a jock (athlete). He was not in the social structure of any of the groups at school. He was as close to a high school misfit as one could get.

One time after PE class, we had just finished showering and were getting dressed for our next class.

David was being his typical awkward self, and another student — I'll call him "Robby" — started picking on him, being very cruel. David was no physical threat to anyone; in every respect, he was an easy target. I told Robby to leave David alone.

By now Robby had an audience, and said to me, "Okay, do you want to fight?"

I replied, "No, not really. But if that is what you need to leave David alone, let's go for it." I added, "Rather than fight in here, with this concrete floor and the wooden benches, let's go into the gym, where the wrestling mats will ensure nobody gets hurt."

With a growing crowd following us, Robby and I took the fight to the gym — but then the PE teacher came out of his office and asked, "What are you guys doing?" We told him. He said, "You cannot fight in the gym. Take it outside." So we took it outside.

Now we had an even larger crowd. We laid into each other. I came out of that fight in pretty good shape, just a little dirt on my shirt; Robby did not do so well, had a bloody nose from where I punched him several times. None of Robby's punches ever connected with me.

Fortunately, the PE teacher finally realized there could be some liability issues, and that he carried some risk for knowing about the fight; he came outside and stopped it. He sent both of us to the vice principal's office; we waited in the outer office.

Mr. Veach was known as a stern disciplinarian. I had never seen him before under these circumstances, had never been in a fight in high school before. First, Mrs. Hoyt, the office manager, asked me what had happened; Robby was in another part of the office. I told her my side of the story. Mrs. Hoyt went into Mr. Veach's office, spoke a bit, then came back out. She said, "Go home and change your shirt." I did. Very soon after, I came back to the office and sat down again. Mrs. Hoyt came out again, looked at me, and said, "Go back to class." I went back to class.

That was it. I never even met with anyone else, never got *"a good talking to,"* never had any other consequence. That would be unheard of today! There would have been multiple meetings, conferences, documents to fill out, and on and on!

The only consequence after was that all the kids who usually got picked on and teased by others would just hang out with me at lunch. Maybe they felt like they had a "guardian angel" in me.

God uses other people to teach or guide us. At times, if we are available, He will use us to be "angels" to other people. This is what it means to me to be filled with — or to walk in — the Spirit of God. It is God's Holy Spirit that influences us beyond our more typical human responses. He uses us to "minister" to other people, like David.

I was learning to respond to God's compassion.

Chapter 12: **ANGELS IN THE WORK PLACE**

In my late 20s, I was working as an assistant principal in a high school. It was a rural community with about 850 students in Grades 9 through 12. Part of the assignment included ample amounts of student discipline; that was my responsibility. It's a challenging job, but I approached these as "teachable moments" for young people, and sometimes for their parents too.

One day I was sitting down for a Parent/Teacher Conference with a mother whose son was being short-term suspended for fighting. This wasn't his first disciplinary hearing, as he wasn't making the best choices. Often the consequences for discipline were make-up assignments or temporary suspension; mostly we did not want students to miss much school.

The meeting started harshly. Before I could barely greet the mother, she started filling the air with curses and accusations, complaints that we were picking on her son, that we were out to get him, and so on. It was brutal.

When facing this type of hostility, there is often a chemical reaction: *"fight or flight."* In this instance, I attribute my different reaction to the work of the Holy Spirit inside of me — rather than rise to her anxiety and hostility, I was quiet and calm, and just let her rage on. After a few minutes, when she realized I was not reacting to her, she began to slow down a bit, and finally came to a pause. She said, "Well, aren't you going to say something?"

Now, while she was yelling at me, I was asking God what was really happening here. He gave me the words, so I said, "This is really hard for you. You love your son, and you are afraid for his safety." At that point, she sat down, her shoulders fell and she began crying quietly. In a few moments, we were talking levelly about what we all could do and, frankly, what she needed to do to get him back on track.

Was there an angel in that room? God's Spirit can use any of us as "an angel" — which, by definition is:

ANGEL: A spiritual being serving as a divine messenger and intermediary, often as a special protector of an individual or nation; an attendant usually benevolent spirit or guardian; part of a person's character or nature, that is said to guide the person's thoughts and behavior.
Merriam-Webster Dictionary

I use "angel" euphemistically, as a person who rises above their own nature and allows God to speak through them to another person in trouble. If we seek His counsel in moments of life that are stressful, very often we will react differently than our natural tendency — that, to me, is "being an angel." Another way to say it is: *"Allowing the Holy Spirit to use me to minister blessings from God to others."* God is always looking for people who will be available to Him; He loves to get involved in His children's lives.

Some people have wondered how or why I would have walked toward working as a public school superintendent for 22 years. It is not a longevity record; I am sure there are others who have fulfilled that role longer — but still, it is a long time to work.

Some have thought I was an ambitious career-climber or motivated by popularity or fame, but, honestly, no one is more surprised than me that I achieved that position. It was never my goal or idea. God used someone else to spark that ambition in me, and do more than make it possible. Here is that story.

Negotiating Life

While still working as a high school assistant principal, I started to think about making a run for a job as a high school principal; that is a fairly normal career path once an assistant principal earns enough experience. At 28 years old, in my first school administrative job, I had started this career path pretty young. Some of the teachers whom I supervised had grown children who were older than me; I imagine it could have been unsettling for them. Still, I had a lot of encouragement to move along, doing administrative work from the classroom, where I was very successful. I guess folks thought if I could do that, then maybe the skill could transfer to a whole school level. Honestly, the most enjoyable job I ever had was as a teacher and a coach, but, Life began to happen differently; or maybe it was God Who was calling me to a different path.

Shortly after the incident with the irate mother, I was in my office when the district superintendent, Paul, came in. He said, "Nick, I would like to talk with you about your career." When the superintendent wants to visit, you don't say no! Paul shared, "Nick, you are doing a really great job. Others have noticed and mentioned to me the leadership skills you have. I have always felt I have the responsibility to encourage others to develop themselves in public Education, even to go into leadership positions. Someone did this with me; I want to pass it forward." I was astonished!

Paul continued, "I have discussed this with the Board of Directors, and we want to offer to pay for part of your doctoral degree, which would enable you to earn your superintendent credentials. This would be in exchange for you committing to stay in this School District for a certain number of years."

I was very flattered, and humbled, and I thanked him for his offer. Then I said, "Thank you, but no! You see, I have a young family; we enjoy being together. I really don't enjoy the academic part of school. I really have no interest in getting a doctoral degree or becoming a superintendent." Paul was polite, and ruefully understanding. He left the offer on the table, and went on his way.

I was busy with work, family and life, without paying much attention to furthering my education. I had earned my Bachelor of Education degree and then my Master's; I had a good job, was growing my family, and was content with what I could see was happening in my life. I did not have a vision or plan beyond the life I was living at that time. There was no role-modeling or discussions with my family in my early life that positioned me to look or think that far ahead.

A year later, Paul showed up again at my office. He said, "I'm back to make the same offer, but this time we, the Board and I, are prepared to increase the amount we are willing to pay in support of you getting your Doctorate, superintendent credentials, and you committing to stay in the District for a specific number of years." This time I was blown away, as I wasn't expecting the first offer nor this second offer a year later. It wasn't that I was negotiating; rather, something inside of me was saying I should take more time and reflect on the offer. I asked Paul for a few days to think it over and get back to him.

For most people, they have trusted family members to turn to for the purpose of making big life choices. That wasn't going to be much help to me, as I've already shared in this book. But over the years, I had developed my own "council of wise people." They were comprised of former teachers, coaches, pastors, friends — people whom I respected and whom I felt had an interest in me as a person, regardless of my utility in their lives.

I ran this second offer past all of them. All of them said I should take the offer to pursue my education as long as I could balance the rigors of the program with my family life and while working full-time.

Still, I was reluctant to take that step. I really enjoyed being physically active, and the idea of sitting again in a classroom was not that appealing. Finally, I created this test (Christians call this *"laying a fleece"*; see Judges 6) of three things that needed to happen; I prayed that if God **really** wanted me to do this, these things would happen:

(1) My wife and I had made an offer of $80,000 on a house that was valued considerably more (this was all we could afford). I asked God to favor us with this house.

(2) Getting into this particular Doctoral program that Paul wanted me to take, was very competitive; I

needed to be accepted — and in that political climate, white males were not commonly accepted over other ethnic candidates.

(3) I needed to feel God calling me on the inside to do this, as it was going to take a lot of time and work. I needed His assurance. [14]

Within several days, the contractor agreed to sell us the house, even though he had higher offers. I don't understand that at all, but he did.

I applied and was accepted into the Doctoral program. Yes, I began to feel God's peace settling inside of me.

This was not my plan, but I was being recruited into something, and sometimes there comes a point when Life is ours to accept, to implement, and not to continue to question. Paul, and those Board Members, and the house contractor, and even the College application staff — were they all part of some plan God was orchestrating for a life I was yet to see?

Their support was life-changing for me; without that, I would not have moved along the path toward being a superintendent. And as it has happened, in my 22 years in that role, I too have encouraged and mentored a number of younger administrators to move forward in their careers. Often I have thought of Paul's encouragement: *"I have always felt I have the responsibility to encourage others to develop themselves in public Education, even to go into leadership positions. Someone did this with me; I want*

---

[14] See Psalm 34:37-, 23-24

to pass it forward." Paul said he needed to grow leadership, and so I have sought to carry that on as much as I could.

Were angels at work, through other people, helping to open those doors and make the way clear? We know that Life happens. We don't always understand or see how or why at times. "Let it be" is what we must do, but knowing and trusting that God is always up to something good on our behalf — this is our peace in all things. It is also our source of courage and motivation, especially in the face of adversity.

> *God will command His angels concerning you, to guard you in all your ways; they will lift you up in their hands, so that you will not strike your foot against a stone.*
> **Psalm 91:11-12**

Work and Dealing With Problems

The Doctoral program was a lot of work, but it was also very interesting. I made great professional friendships with others in that class, and finished the program and earned my degree within the three years scheduled. I was focused on getting it done, so much so that my class-mates affectionately called me *"RoboDoc."* I had to give up some sunny weekends of water-skiing; and once, Alisa, my then-four-year-old daughter, asked her Mom, "Does Daddy live in Seattle?" (I was away from home one weekend per month plus one night per week). Still, we all survived.

I remained in that school district and honored my time commitment. I also moved from the school to the District level as an administrator. I learned more directly from Paul about the work of the superintendent. At age 34, I applied for my first superintendent job, and was hired. I remained in that District for 10 years, then moved on to the more recent District, where I worked for 12 years before retiring.

There are many stories, experiences and insights to share after this length of time as a school superintendent; I am saving those for another time. This is not *that* book.

In my mid-50s, it was time for me to have my right shoulder replaced. I knew it was coming because a few years prior I had the left shoulder replaced; the doctor said my shoulder issue was on both sides; apparently it was some type of genetic malfunction.

I have "flat glenoids" — bone crevices which are supposed to be cupped in a shape so that the ball (the head of the humerus bone which tops the arm) can rotate nicely in that pocket. Having flat pockets rather than cupped pockets — and then doing all these activities like weight-lifting, snow-skiing, water-skiing — had eventually worn the balls of the humerus bone to where they rubbed the glenoid into flat, gnarly knobs, causing limited movement, which was very painful. This was the problem on both shoulders, and I needed replacement parts.

I have always been active, even later in life into my 50s, and these joint challenges were issues I was not going to surrender to — I had no intention of taking up a "slower lifestyle." That day will come; however, as long as I have a way to address to stay active, I am going to fight to keep moving.

I've also had a two-level fusion of my lower spine; this was even before the shoulder problems. That repair took place when I was in my mid-40s; the doctor said it likely happened in my early 20s, from playing Football. That procedure had gone well, and I was even water-skiing four months to the day after that surgery. I'm the proud owner of two steel plates, six screws, a carbon-filter box, and two columns of fused bone; the doctor did a great job. I was a good patient, worked hard at rehabilitation, and while there was some pain associated with it, it was nothing compared to the pain of the shoulders' procedures.

There are different types of shoulder replacement surgery. The procedure I selected involved the doctor using a tool to grind (ream) a cup-shape directly into the flat glenoid area of the bone. He then removed the gnarly, worn head of the humerus and replaced it with a nice, smooth ball that fit into the new "cup." By not using any plastic inserts on the cup side, this procedure allows the body to gradually generate calcium in the joint, which keeps it tight. Once healed, the patient should be able to resume full activity levels. And so it did. I still water-ski and snow-ski, even with having both shoulders replaced; I still lift weights as part of my normal work-out routine. I have no issues with my back or either of my shoulders.

In the Operating Room

There is a catch, however, to shoulder replacement surgery: this procedure requires that the patient move and use the repaired joint immediately. Even being wheeled out of the operating room after the procedure, they have already hooked up a device that keeps the shoulder moving. This is extremely painful. At some point, the pain-killing medications are not equal to the pain — and this rehab movement has to happen for weeks, even months. When the muscles and components are eventually healed, the patient can start adding resistance to improve exercise and build back strength.

Sorry, I didn't mean to write an entire medical book. My point is that when I knew I would need to have the right shoulder replaced, I remembered from the left shoulder procedure that it was going to require another tough rehab. It wasn't entirely a slam-dunk decision; in addition to basic anxiety about having another major surgery, there is always the risk one has to weigh — on one hand, the risk of doing something that requires surgery … and on the other hand, not doing something and then living with that outcome. My decision was, *"As long as they have replacement parts, and my medical insurance covers it, then I am going to stay active and keep this body moving."* I am in better health as a result, so the only hesitation or anxiety about the second shoulder surgery was in the long, hard road of recovery.

About three weeks before the operation, I had a very vivid dream. In the dream I could see myself laying on the surgical table in the operating room, surrounded by doctors and nurses. Standing by my head was a very large, very strong, very powerful-looking doctor, wearing surgical gear. Suddenly, he revealed angelic wings that spread wide open; he leaned over me, and covered my entire body with his wings. The medical staff were continuing with their work, unseeing of the wings or the "doctor." I was completely comfortable, calm, safe during the procedure, in the arms and under the wings of this angel. That sense of safety and peace, I recall very clearly.

The next day, I told my wife about the dream. I interpreted it as God's way of saying I was going to be fine.

The day appointed for the surgery arrived. I was at the hospital doing check-in and all the pre-operation routines. This included different people talking with me, marking my shoulder, asking questions, showing me where to change out of my street clothes and into a surgical gown, reading my ID bracelet; all that. In all the bustle, I noticed a tall, strong, handsome doctor standing in the room. He had a small smile on his face; he appeared to be overseeing everyone. Then he made eye contact with me, and gave me a calming, reassuring look.

Something about his presence was different. He wasn't doing any of the tasks the other medical personnel were doing. I asked him, "What is your role in this procedure?"

He replied, "I am on rotation; this is part of my training." I assumed he meant a rotation related to some medical school. I left it at that, and in a few minutes, I was being rolled into the operating room, still wide awake.

I don't take any anesthesia until the last minute as the drugs they give to make me relax also make me nauseous; this I had learned from previous surgeries. So while I was in the operating room, I was actually helping them hold the mask to my face as they prepared for the procedure. I lay back on the bed ...

and at that moment, I looked above my head and — to my surprise — saw this same *"just observing doctor"* standing above me, looking at me. He had the same reassuring smile of the angel in my dream — and I recalled from the dream that he was now standing in exactly the same place as the angel had been. In that moment, I felt exactly the same way — comforted, calm, safe, peaceful — as I had in the dream. I sensed that the same angel was standing over me in surgery and would be covering me with his wings.

Then they started the anesthetic drugs and I began counting backward from 100. I never remember how far I get in that counting! The next thing I remember was waking up ... and soon after that, having my just-repaired arm placed in the device that makes it move. Yeah, ouch!

To this day, I still don't know if that person was really a doctor or an angel-in-training. Maybe he really was doctor-in-training and somehow was assigned to observe my surgical procedure. Maybe God used someone to make me feel secure like I did in the dream, someone who would stand in that exact place on the day of my surgery.

Before leaving the hospital, I asked one of the nurses who was on the prep team. She mentioned various people, but did not recall that person. I never saw a name tag! Draw your own conclusions; I was there.

Do not forget to show hospitality to strangers, for by so doing, some people have shown hospitality to angels without knowing it.

Hebrews 13:2

Who has been an angel is your life? For whom are you an angel? Are you available for God to use on a moment's notice, to be part of something larger and more important? There's a world of people in need around us! We can see a large crowd of people — but in that crowd there are individuals, with their own stories, happening in real time. Can you be part of their stories in a way that touches them and leaves them somehow in a better way? Are you available to God in this way?

Chapter 13: **OF VISIONS AND DREAMS**

God's Directions for Life are not difficult to find:

> *"In the last days," God says, "I will pour out My Spirit on all people. Your sons and daughters will prophesy;* **your young men will see visions, your old men will dream dreams.** *Even on My servants, both men and women, I will pour out My Spirit in those days, and they will prophesy."*
>
> **Acts 2:17-18**; emphasis added

"Your young men will see visions, and your old men will dream dreams." There are a variety of ways God gets our attention. The purpose is often to teach us something relevant to our growth and development in the directions He wants us to achieve. Here are some of the unique experiences I have had in this respect.

Like many people, my wife and I like to go out for dinner. Usually, it's nothing fancy, and we often vary the destination just to try different places. It is relaxing to have someone else prepare the meal, and it gives us an opportunity to keep the "courtship" part of our relationship going in marriage, especially with the often-fast pace of life.

In dreams, God uses things with which we are familiar as the scaffolding for what He wants to teach us.

Dinner At the Mansion

One night, I was sound asleep, and dreaming my wife and I were going out for dinner. Nothing too exciting or profound, right? But as we walked in the door to this restaurant, I knew we had never been there before. The restaurant was in a large mansion, with a grand entry, rich wood décor, and a long, regal staircase that gently wound itself from the landing upward to a large banquet room on the floor above. The smell of wonderful food wafted down, and there was a sense of a festive, friendly atmosphere in that banquet room. In a way, it was like we would be meeting family and friends; at the same time, they were not people we knew by name.

Standing at the foot of the staircase was the Host. He was a well-groomed man, appropriately attired, as he greeted the guests and led them to their tables upstairs in the banquet room. As we walked toward the Host, he looked up and smiled, welcoming us. He eloquently asked, "Table for two?"

I replied, "Yes, thank you." Then, abruptly, it occurred to me that I had no idea of the cost of this obviously fine dinner. When we usually select a place to dine out, we may not know the exact cost but we will have a sense of it. In my dream, I was keenly aware that we had never been to this restaurant before; we were not familiar with it, so it seemed like a reasonable query to make. I asked, "What is the cost of this meal?"

The Host urbanely replied, "Twenty-five thousand dollars."

"$25,000?!? For dinner?"

He calmly answered, "Yes, sir."

"Well, I'm sure it is a nice dinner, but there is no way I can pay $25,000 for a dinner."

The Host moved closer to me; now I could see His face clearly. He asked, "Nick, would you pay $25,000 to have dinner with Me?" — for now I saw that the Host was Jesus Christ.

Immediately I was humbled, and with a flood of emotion, I gasped, "Lord, I would pay $50,000 — and give **everything** that I have — to have dinner with You!"

Then the dream ended. That was it.

An interesting aspect of this dream, is that it came at a time in my life when I was struggling and trying to sort out the general idea of financial giving (charitable donations). *"How much to give and to what causes?"* had been on my mind; I was in a place of seeking guidance and direction. That dream really gave me pause to consider how much we spend on recreational things, in contrast to the giving to those less fortunate than us — those whom God loves dearly, those who will always be with us and need our support.

This dream was not Jesus telling us to not go out for dinner. He was not saying we should avoid recreation. He was gentle, and even used humor in this dream — but it was personal and clear to me that He was saying, "Nick, when you see those who are less fortunate and are wondering about giving, do so as if you are doing it for Me." It changed my perceptions about giving; it changed the way I look at people who are in need. It changed me.

The Charlatan

In another dream, I was in a church. There was a religious-looking person wearing a long dark gown and a high-crested hat, who was telling everyone in the church that he knew *"the right way to God,"* that he had special powers and everyone should follow him. There was a bird on the rafter above him, and every now and then the speaker would point to his regal hat … and the bird would fly to it, then fly back to its perch on the rafter.

This person told everyone that the bird obeying him was a sign of his power, and that even all the birds everywhere would obey him. As I listened, my spirit began to rise up, elevating me enough that I could see into the top of this man's hat. There were cracker crumbs on the hat, and when he pointed to them, the bird would fly down to snatch a bit of cracker.

It was nothing more than a magician's trick. Perhaps it was a well-trained bird, and possibly a good trick on the "religious man's" part, but clearly it was not real, not authentic; it was designed to mislead people from a healthy walk with God. I tried to tell the congregation that this guy was a fake, but they were totally charmed and deceived — they believed him.

Then, I was outside the church, and I saw the ghostly torsos of "souls" (departed people) swaying with the gentle wind. As people began to exit the church — and out of houses in the area — they saw these souls, and started freaking out, running, scared, frightened by these spirits.

What they could not discern was that these were the souls of those who had been slain for God; [15] good spirits, gentle and loving. I sensed them ... and they resonated with God's Spirit inside of me. I was not afraid. I tried to tell the people that they should not be afraid of them — rather, to fear the "religious person" who was misleading them. It was he who was causing them to be afraid of these supernatural appearances which they could not understand. I pleaded with them to listen to their hearts — but they were only hearing in their minds, trying to make sense of the supernatural ... but mostly, so invested in this charlatan and the "religion" he was selling, that they missed God in the opportunity completely. It was heart-breaking.

The morning after this dream, there was a very short, very strong message, an interpretation that was quite simple: *"Nick, follow Me and not Man's religion."* **Got it!**

I know **there is great value in learning about God.** I am not anti-church or anti-religion, but we must be very careful to learn from others yet not make them become our "god" or take the place of God — that can lead to missing the direct connection we have with God. He will work directly in your life, in your heart, and He will use many different ways to connect with you.

> *It is by the Name of Jesus Christ of Nazareth, Who was crucified but Whom God raised from the dead, that this man stands before you healed. Jesus is "the Stone that the builders rejected, which has become the Cornerstone."*

---

[15] See Revelation 6:9-11.

Salvation is found in no one else, for there is no other Name under Heaven given to Mankind by which we must be saved.

Acts 4:10-14; emphasis added

(also see John 14:6)

The "Secret" of This Book

Another similar dream God used featured a man from my past who means a great deal to me; his name was Mr. O'Brien, and he has passed from this Life. He was the PE teacher who had invited me into his office in middle school when I was hanging out with the "wrong gang." I really admired him.

In the dream, Mr. O'Brien came and — although I knew he has passed and he was speaking to me from Heaven — I thought it was pretty cool, in the dream, to be hearing from him. He came to me in this dream on behalf of God. He said, "There's some really big stuff coming ahead, and we're going to need you!" It was like he was giving me a pep talk before a big Football game, asking if I was willing to play.

I was pumped up and motivated: "Yeah, Coach! I am ready! Put me in the game and let me at 'em!"

He said, "Great, but before you do that, I need you to get a can of soda pop for me." He indicated that he wanted me to go to a different place from where we were, to a different building. I was perplexed.

I thought it was odd for me to go chasing after that can of soda pop, when there was this much more important thing coming up. But then I thought, *"Well, I'll just be humble, be a servant, and do whatever he asks me to do."* So I went running through the building to get that can of soda pop for Mr. O'Brien. I was still highly motivated to do that big thing; I figured I would find the can of soda pop and bring it back to him in a few moments, and then I would get to be in the big thing that was about to happen. **That** was *really* the Heavenly assignment I was being prepared for … *right?*

I found the place where I could get the soda pop for Mr. O'Brien. Except there was a long line of people already there, and I was going to have to wait in line, to be patient before I would get the soda pop and finally deliver on my Earthly task before I headed into the Heavenly assignment. This didn't really upset me, but I was trying to reconcile my motivation to "just get it done and move on" with this waiting in line stuff.

The dream was beginning to fade, and I was waking up! I was frustrated just standing in some stupid line and not getting into the big thing I was being asked to do. As I was between sleeping and waking, I prayed for some insight, some way to make sense out of this strange dream. I heard a Voice:

"Nick, love the people in line!"

"No way!" part of me wanted to scream, because I'm not patient, and I really like to play hard. But then I said, "Yes, Lord, show me how to help, and use me when You need me." And then I knew the meaning of the dream.

Life is a lot about waiting in line, and looking at the people in line … and helping the people in line. And loving the people in line. There was a time when I thought that the only way to really serve God was for all of us to move to some Third World country and find some "path" of service in order to be useful and helpful to God. At this moment in my life, through this dream, it was revealed to me that the "correctness" of a "path" in Life is not so much in the path itself **but in how we walk the path we are on, and for whom.**

It really is about loving God and loving others, as we love ourselves, and about doing that where we are here and now. Love God ... and love people.

> *"Love the Lord your God with all your heart, and with all your soul, and with all your strength, and with all your mind"* and *"Love your neighbor as yourself."*
>
> **Luke 10:27**

We don't have to move to some other place to do this, to be this person. We **can** move there — and there may be times when we are lead or called to literally "change paths," in this respect — but most often God will put us in a place, or can use us in a place, where we are at any time. If we are open and receptive to this with Him and in our hearts, if we are available for Him to use to touch others' lives.

This dream came when I had been really deep in the Word of God (the Bible) and was feeling amazingly close and soft-hearted in my walk with God. There was a tugging in my spirit, a longing to be "Home in Heaven," that was very strong. I don't dislike life on Earth — there are many things about life that are beautiful and worth doing ... and I also like people (well, most of them) — so it's not that I want to die and be gone. There is a balance between our longing for

Heaven and being with God, fully focused on Him ... and an availability to be with people where we are placed in our life time, on this Earth, in the time and location where we have been placed.

God wants YOU and ME to love the people who are in line with us

Each of us, as Christians, are being prepared for Eternity — and we need to be good students in that preparation — still, we need to be present in this Life, to help those in front of us and those behind us, while we are all waiting in line.

This was an important message for me because, at times in my life, I hardly even saw the people in line. Now, God wants me to love them! It's not a passive perspective — it's an active assignment!

Learning About Forgiveness

Later in this book, I share about my journey with advanced pancreatic cancer. I am in a "life extension" mode now, as — short of a miracle — this disease is not curable. As you will also read later, God is with me, and while I am doing my best to stay vertical, I am at peace. My prayer is simply for His will to be done with me, and that I do my part well. So, there have been some dreams and messages God has given me during the cancer journey that are appropriate to share in this chapter. Here they are:

I had been struggling with the difference between my head knowledge of being forgiven through Jesus' death and resurrection, with my personal emotions of just not feeling worthy. I replay the tapes of my own life, my choices, my actions, etc., and I have not always done the right thing. In fact, I have made more poor choices at times that hurt others. It was not my intent to hurt them, but — by being selfish or self-sufficient — it had that effect. I was not, and am not, perfect, and I recall those things I wish I would have done differently. I know I am saved, but did not "feel saved" as I focused on my shortcomings. Have you ever been in that place of doubt?

So, one night as I slept, in this dream I was standing before God, and showing Him this conflict between my head and my heart. And I was feeling unworthy, for sure! Then, God the Father's Voice said, *"I won't call you out."*

Then came the interpretation. God was saying that when I come to Heaven, He wasn't going to call attention to my sins — rather, He wanted to call attention to **what His Son, Jesus, had done for me** and others, in terms of forgiveness. Salvation isn't about "earning" it — it is about **the gifts of grace and mercy** that we can claim only through what Jesus did for us.

The other thing so powerful in this dream was the tone of voice God used. It was that of a Father Who was justifiably proud of what His Son, Jesus, had done for us. So much so that God has deferred to Jesus who "gets in" and who does not. We are so fortunate that Jesus lived as a human too, because He can advocate for us because He has walked in our shoes!

Since that dream, I both know I am forgiven, and I **feel** it now too. God answers our heartfelt prayers.

On another night, the dream found me in a college library. I was in a certain class which had an assignment to write a paper — but I didn't know what the topic or theme was. So I was asking others in the class, but nobody was helpful. Finally, one friend said, "Nick, the assignment is write about your most challenging situation in life, and how you got through it."

I thought, *"Well, that's it: the most challenging situation would be dealing with cancer, and telling how God is sustaining me through the treatments and everything."* At the same time, I was also questioning whether it was even wise to be taking a class during the cancer ordeal. I was thinking about dropping the class, or not take it for credit, or not try to get a good grade, and so forth. It was unsettling.

I forged ahead and finished the assignment, and was about to turn it in to the teacher of the class. I am "old school": I was actually heading to the teacher's office with paper in hand, not sending it via e-mail or anything. I arrived at the teacher's desk and held out my paper. He reached out and held both of my hands … and it was Jesus — He was the Teacher!

Jesus said, "Nick, don't worry about passing this class or your grades. I will teach you what you need to know, and — when it gets hard — I will be with you to get you through it." Then, with a warm smile and a kind, reassuring voice, even some gentle humor as He accepted my assignment, He said, "By the way, you will get a good grade and full credit."

He leaned back at His desk and said, "Now, let's see what you wrote." I know it sounds silly, but life with God is about doing our best for Him in every situation, and trusting Him for the rest.

"If Heaven Never Was Promised to Me" [16]

When one has a terminal illness, and the prospect of death is imminent, it can raise a great many questions as to what life might be like after this life. For me, and others who are saved by the grace of God, Heaven is a promise. Yet, what happens in Heaven?

My idea of Heaven was, frankly, not that exciting. I love God, mind you, but have a hard time with many church services. I probably figured Heaven would be more along those lines: singing, standing, sitting, praying, listening, more singing, more praying. So I figured, much like reading travel brochures before embarking on a trip, "If I am going to die, it would be best to do some research, read some books about Heaven."

I read the book, *"Heaven"* by Randy Alcorn [17] and *"All Things New"* by John Eldridge [18]. Both are very well done, based on Biblical truths that really helped expand my view, amend some misconceptions, and raise anticipation of Heaven. During this time, God blessed me with another dream — a glimpse of Heaven, just to put my heart at ease.

---

[16] *"If Heaven Never Was Promised to Me"* is a song written by Andraé Crouch; copyright © 1973; all rights reserved; used with permission

[17] *"Heaven"* by Randy Alcorn; copyright © 2011; published by Tyndale House Publishers.

[18] *"All Things New"* by John Eldridge; copyright © 2017; published by HarperCollins Publishers.

In this dream, a friend and I had finished some work we were doing together, then drove out of a park-like setting. We saw a lake surrounded by trees, and drove to that spot. When I got out, I knew this was not a place I had ever seen before on Earth. The lake was contained by large, beautiful rock walls, edging the lake so it looked like an infinity pool, with water cascading over the sides. I walked under these little waterfalls, then walked up to the lake which was about twelve feet higher.

It was a very large body of water. There were beautiful homes nestled into the trees on one side; I could see warm light from inside the homes. Across the lake, snow-covered mountains bordered the other side, leading to the water. It was glorious.

There were people there who knew me, although I did not recognize exactly who they were; one showed me around. I waded into the lake water, expecting it to be cold — it wasn't! It was the perfect temperature. Standing in the lake, I looked up at the sky, and realized the stars were not strewn randomly but rather, were neatly organized into different geometric shapes. I began to realize that God was telling me, *"This isn't Earth."*

I thought, *"Who owns this place? It is so beautiful."* I turned to my friend and said, "Maybe we shouldn't be walking around here if this is private property!" My friend just smiled and relaxed in a chair under a tree. As I was marveling about all this strange beauty, my dream began to fade and I started to come out of it. Before the dream was gone, I asked God, "Who owns this property?"

He said, "It is shared."

What I had read in those books about Heaven were resonating in my head. I replied, "This is fine." God spoke directly to my heart — He is like that, you know.

It was about this same time that I was praying about Heaven, and thinking about my Dad and my brother Scott. They were not people whom I really liked, for obvious reasons, but I didn't want them to go to Hell. As I was praying, asking God about how to understand how this is dealt with in Heaven, I felt like He said: *"Don't worry, Nick. Heaven is really big."*

Chapter 14: **HOLY WATER**

Some say that people see their lives flash before their eyes when they are about to die or are having a near-death experience. I had a dream where this happened, but I was neither dying nor near death.

In my dream, a slideshow of images from my past — all the events up to my age, which at that time was in my early 40s — was playing rapidly. Then the images stopped moving, and I felt my soul draining out of my body, like water draining out of a broken glass. Yet, my soul, my being, was being supported by the water that was flowing out of my body — it was less a loss of water than a joining of my water with other waters all around me. I felt my water merging into rivers, lakes, even rain. I could sense the presence of other souls in the merging water, which felt "clean."

Clean water seemed to hold "loving souls," yet there was also dirty water — harsh, troubled, unclean — that was holding "unloving souls." The difference was startling.

The Bible mentions water frequently; in Creation, God worked with water right from the start (see Genesis 1:1-9). When Jesus Christ shared about water, it was epic (see John 4:1-42). Jesus referred to Himself as *"the Living Water,"* and spoke of water on many accounts, both the real and symbolic values of water for all living beings.

Wouldn't it be interesting if the place where God holds the souls of those departed was "in water"? That might explain much about water's capacity to sustain life — and our desperate situation without water, in particular, "Living Water." Consider how many times, and in many different ways, water is used in the Bible, in religious practice, and in life. Water is significant for baptism, cleaning, sustaining life. Water flowed from Jesus when He was pierced by the soldier after He had died on the cross. [19]

Water was the source of life for Noah and his family (and all the livestock) safely floating on the Ark; and yet water was the death of those who refused to believe God (see Genesis 6 through 9). The infant Moses was floated to safety on the water of the Nile River (see Exodus 2:1-10), so he could go on to fulfill God's deliverance from Egypt. The water of the Red Sea became the cut-off point for the Egyptian army pursuing the Hebrews (see Exodus 14), wiping out the soldiers who were sent to capture them. Life-saving water flowed from the rock at Moses' command when the people were dying in the wilderness (see Exodus 17).

Centuries later, Jesus walks on water (see Matthew 14:29-31) to join His disciples; and He had control over stormy water (see Mark 6:50-51) and rescued His frightened disciples. The examples of water in the Bible go on and on; see John 7:38-39; Isaiah 12:3; Revelation 22:1-2; Ezekiel 47:9; Jeremiah 17:13; Zechariah 14:8-9. Water is a big deal to us and is a big deal in History. It is significant in the Bible, and will be in our future as well. [20]

---

[19] See John 19:31-35

[20] See Isaiah 55:1-2; also Revelation 22:17

All Water is Holy!

In John 4, there is a beautiful and powerful exchange when Jesus speaks with a woman at Jacob's Well, showing her concepts of thirst, water for human life, and the Living Water of Life that quenches our thirst for Eternity. It's worthwhile reading the whole passage together:

Now Jesus had to go through Samaria. So He came to a town in Samaria called Sychar, near the plot of ground Jacob had given to his son Joseph. Jacob's Well was there; and Jesus, tired as He was from the journey, sat down by the Well. It was about noon. When a Samaritan woman came to draw water, Jesus said to her, "Will you give Me a drink?" (His disciples had gone into the town to buy food.)

The Samaritan woman said to Him, "You are a Jew and I am a Samaritan woman. How can You ask me for a drink?" (For Jews do not associate with Samaritans.)

Jesus answered her, "If you knew the gift of God and Who it is that asks you for a drink, you would have asked Him, and He would have given you Living Water."

"Sir," the woman said, "You have nothing to draw with and the Well is deep. Where can You get this Living Water?" Are You greater than our father Jacob, who gave us the Well and drank from it himself, as did also his sons and his livestock?"

Jesus answered, "Everyone who drinks this water will be thirsty again, but whoever drinks the Water I give them will never thirst. Indeed, the Water I give them will become in them a Spring of Water welling up to Eternal Life."
John 4:4-14; emphasis added

Here's the background. Jesus was making a long walk from one city to another, and His body was tired, and thirsty. He stops at a very famous well in Samaria to rest, to have a drink ... and to deliver an important message. This message was given to a certain Samaritan woman, but it is a message given to all of us.

There were other wells where Jesus could have stopped along the way, but Jacob's Well was significant in that time and culture. It was attributed to have been found and dug by an important Old Testament person, Jacob, whose lineage was responsible for all the Hebrew race. By selecting Jacob's Well as the location for this story to happen, Jesus was symbolically connecting God's new promise of Eternal Life and relationship with God in the spiritual, through Jesus, "the Living Water" — with a physical, tangible, practical source of water for day-to-day life. It should not be overlooked that Jesus chose this particular, significant Well for such an important revelation announcement.

Jesus is also connecting with a Samaritan woman, what was unusual on two fronts: (a) Jews traditionally were in a long-standing dispute with Samaritans, and so did not associate with them at all, if they could avoid it; and (b) men did not speak to women at all, especially to a stranger (although they spoke with women of their own families). Jesus was breaking two old "rules" in order to establish a new "rule": everyone can now partake of Living Water! Jesus was offering Living Water freely to everyone, regardless of their Man-made social structures or restrictions.

There's a lot of "Samaritan woman" in all of us, especially in our attempts to find life through many choices and many actions we take, apart from God. This woman was profoundly off-track; she was living with her fifth man — just replace "the man" with any type of substitute: people, places, things, hyper-activities, habits, diversions, distractions — things that each us have used or still use to "quench our thirst." Our challenge comes not so much from the things we can see but from the things we cannot see, the blind spots that exist in our lives.

"Can You See Me Now?"

When my two older kids, Alisa and Kyle, were learning to drive, I figured out a way to help improve their skills, their awareness of this big new piece of machinery that we were about to trust into their inexperienced hands. It started with (for instance) Alisa getting into the car parked in the garage, rolling down all the windows, and adjusting the mirrors (center rear-view, driver's on the left-side, passenger's on the right-side) — but the motor turned off. I was outside the car. For this exercise, she was to use **only** the mirrors to locate me in the mirror.

At first, I stood in front of the car and asked, "Can you see me now?"

Alisa grinned and said deprecatingly, "Daaad! Come on, of course I can see you, you're right in front of me."

So I moved to stand beside the right-side passenger door, and asked, "Can you see me now?"

Alisa laughed, "Dad, I can still see you through the side window!" That was not the point of the exercise.

So I moved to stand behind the right-side passenger door, and asked, "Can you see me now?"

Peering only at the right-side mirror, Alisa replied, "Yes, I can see you."

I moved to the right rear of the car, and asked her, "Can you see me now?" First trying the right-side mirror, then the rear-view mirror, she said, "No."

I said, "This is a blind spot." Next I stepped directly behind the car, asked, "Can you see me now?" Alisa went back to the rear-view mirror and turned it until she could see me. She gave me a thumbs-up.

Next I stepped behind the left side of the car, near the left back corner, and asked, "Can you see me now?"

Now Alisa switched her gaze to the left-side mirror, and she said, "I can hear you. I know you are there, but I cannot see you!"

I said again, "This is a blind spot." One step at a time, I moved all around the perimeter of the car, asking over and over, "Can you see me now?"

What Alisa soon discovered is that **all cars have "blind spots"**: places where she could **hear** my voice but not see me or my image. From that blind spot, I explained, "I could be a car, or a truck, or a motorcycle, or a dumpster. With only mirrors, you can't see into those blind spots." The only way Alisa could know for certain where I was, required her to not trust completely in what she saw (or didn't see) in the mirrors — in order to find me, she had to turn her head and look.

That is how I taught my kids to understand that we all have blind spots. This was especially important as new drivers, but there's a bigger application too.

So often our view of the world and our lives is in the mirror — or perspective — shared with us by others, or what we see in our own minds or through our own experiences. These give us different views, but none of them are complete or comprehensive. We can make dangerous mistakes if we interpret Life only via these reflections. God offers to give us His Holy Spirit to guide us from within, to show us where the blind spots are in our lives, and to lead us through all things.

God will show you the blind spots. He is not trying to pound us into the ground, or condemn us; rather, He will reveal to us the things we don't see. Very often, these are behind, or beside, or just around the corner of the things we do see ... and it is the vision or mirror-images that fill our eyes and senses, that distract us often from the things we need to see in those blind spots. Pray about it. Ask Him to show you the things you don't see, that He wants you to see. He will.

Best of all: God wants us to listen for His Voice … and then turn around and look at Him right in the Face. He is right there, with a smile as big as a Father's, waiting for us. He is.

Chapter 15: **GOD'S WAYS VERSUS MAN'S WAYS**

My entry into college life was a little different than the student who goes to school mostly for the Academic interests. I was going as a result of a Football scholarship, or perhaps would not have gone at all. My experiences with Football would reinforce some aspects of my life, and at the same time it would be in that setting that God would begin to transform my heart to set down Football as that "god" and find a walk closer with Him.

I was successful in the program and, as a freshman, was moved from Running Back to Defensive Back, with the head coach's vision for me to become a starting Strong Safety by my sophomore year.

There were a lot of neat people in the program; and there were also people who made my spirit cringe. I won't name names or go into detail, but I simply felt so isolated; at least, the part of me that mattered most to me, did not feel "at home" at all in that setting. This isn't a story or a slam on college Football — it was my experience, and in part, how I viewed those experiences at that time in my life.

I started to realize how people were treated differently. Understand that at most major vniversities, Football is a big business. Yes, it is a big sport, with a great deal of interest and support, but understand that the proceeds from this one sport, in many cases, provide financial support for many others activities in the college setting.

Within this, there was also differentiation in how athletes were treated. Treatment of people related directly to an athlete's value to the team or program. If one guy was viewed in a positive light, there were many perks and better interactions with other players and coaches. If, however, a player was not as effective on the Football field, this negatively impacted his treatment away from the field.

I even got to know a great guy, a senior, who never really bloomed as a player in that program. He was worried they were going to take away the fourth year of his scholarship due to him not playing at a sufficiently high level. I wondered if they could or would really do that to him? They used me to recruit Christian athletes, but for other recruits who had different reputations, they found guys on the team to take them to parties.

The longer I was around the program and saw these things, the more it ate at me on in the inside. Playing Football was not the problem — those moments were pure and expressive. But those times were being overrun, overcome by this growing incongruence of my core values, and the values that were being reinforced by many in and around the program. As I had previously experienced with my Dad: *"They talked the talk but they didn't walk the walk."*

From a rational, logical perspective, it was obvious that, in time, we all would have to give up the game; either from injury, competition, or age, there would be a point where Football in our lives would reach an end. I wondered if it might be best to accept this, to address it some way that would result in me making a decision to do whatever was going to happen after Football. Exactly **what** that "life after Football" was or would be,

I honestly had no idea, and I felt deeply that I wouldn't be able to answer that question from my present perspective. At the same time, I was progressively convinced that I could not just endure the program and the life I was living and still "connect the dots" without a sense of meaning, purpose and direction.

It's not that I was struggling with my classes; they were fine, and I had a good grade-point average (GPA). In fact, I had one of the highest GPAs on the team. All my costs were being paid for by the scholarship, so the financial issues that unsettle many College students were not my issues. Still, my heart ached — that special place where God lived, was just in pain in those days. Neither was it homesickness — the opposite, actually: I was happier to **not** go home. But inside, I was unhappy and sick.

I even tried going to youth groups, connecting with other players who were Christians too; but they seemed to be okay with everything that was "the program," while I was not at all content. I was not in the right place, and nothing I could do was fixing that incomplete feeling inside.

With hindsight, the best I can explain it is that when we set goals and believe if — or when — we accomplish them, then we will be happy ... but when our goals don't line up with God's goals for our lives, when we "get there," we find it is so empty. It isn't what we imagined it would be. Perhaps we should be learning something about ourselves through this?

Up to this point, my life had been all about Football, and I was reaching my goals in pursuit of this "god" I was serving. I was "getting there," only to realize it was so false on so many levels. I loved playing the game … but now I couldn't see making it my whole life.

As I came to realize that much of the attention received was conditional on performance, not the content of one's inner self, it was confusing and disappointing. My identity was about **what** I could do, not so much **who** I was. I was fortunate to be "good at Football" — and was awarded for that ability — but still I struggled with the basic questions: *"Who am I apart from an athlete? What am I going to do with my life after Football? Apart from being an athlete, who am I, and how will I fill my life? What is my value as a person apart from Football?"* I did not have answers to these questions, and I knew I was not able to answer them where I was at that time.

This won't make a lot of sense to those who have hopes for college and possibly a professional career. I was at the place where I **could have** pursued a pro Football career, but now I was not sure that's what I really wanted. Right there in the beginning of my college years, I was feeling like I needed to leave, to give up my scholarship and, essentially, the Football path I had worked so hard to establish, and was actually on track to complete.

Before I made any firm decisions, I sought the counsel of the pastor of a local church. I shared everything that was going on inside of me; I explained that, from the world's perspective, my concerns made no sense. The pastor just listened. I poured out what I was feeling and thinking about my life, about being in school, just everything.

This pastor looked at me and asked, "How old are you?"

"I'm 19."

He continued, "You are asking questions that I don't usually hear until people are in their 40s. These are real questions about life, and most people don't get around to asking them until they're much older, have more life experience." Perhaps because my early life experiences had been so difficult, maybe I was already "middle-aged" in some ways?

He concluded, "God's ways are not always Man's ways. You need to do what you are being called to do in your heart, even if most people will not understand."

"My thoughts are not your thoughts, neither are your ways My ways," declares the LORD. "As the Heavens are higher than the Earth, so are My ways higher than your ways and My thoughts than your thoughts."

Isaiah 55:8-9

This was a big decision. I knew it would not make sense to many people, those who would evaluate this from the outside, looking into my life. Still, that's where I was, and I knew that in that setting, there was too much incongruence, too much of a difference between what was within me and what was all around me.

I remembered Mabel Thompson, leaning into my face and stating: *"You need to do something important with your life."*

It was growing inside that I needed to do what was necessary to save that part of me that was worth my whole life. I needed to "lose this life" in order to find my life apart from Football, and in some other ways God was leading me.

> Then Jesus said to His disciples, "Whoever wants to be My disciple must deny themselves and take up their cross and follow Me. For whoever wants to save their life will lose it, but whoever loses their life for Me will find it. What good will it be for someone to gain the whole world yet forfeit their soul? Or what can anyone give in exchange for their soul?"
>
> **Matthew 16:24-26**

I made an appointment with the head coach, Jim Walden. I was nervous. He was a good man, and had always been fully supportive. I felt badly because they have invested — literally, through a full scholarship — in me, and while I played mostly junior varsity while still a freshman (so I could learn my position), I knew I was also being observed and expected to make a start, a contribution for the team in the next year. It was not an easy decision.

In his office, I told him my truth: I was leaving the Football program. He did try to make an effort to talk me out of it. He asked me if anything amiss or strange was going on. He arranged for another coach to invite me over for dinner later that week, with the goal of convincing me to stay; I still said I had to leave. I remembered Mrs. Thompson's exhortation to do something important with my life … and felt inside that Football was not it.

On March 16, 1978, I withdrew from college. Actually, I went to classes that morning — as I had never skipped a class before and wasn't going to start then, even though I was going to be leaving the school. In the afternoon, I walked to the Administration building and signed out of college, giving up my scholarship. There was no elaborate plan of what to do next, but I knew I needed to close that one and find another path that would allow my heart to be whole.

I was 19.

Chapter 16: **SITTING ON A LOG IN ALASKA**

Within a couple of weeks, a friend of mine, Chuck, and I were living in the basement of his cousin's house in Seattle. The cousin's husband was a commercial fisherman, so we thought, "Why not!' and started walking around the docks of Fisherman's Wharf, asking various captains if they needed any crew.

We had no experience and honestly did not fully understand the different types of fishing that each boat did for the industry. Still, we wanted an adventure and we needed to make money. After many attempts and just as many turning us down, we both finally landed a job as crew on the same boat.

The *"Gayle Y"* was a 36-foot halibut boat. These are also called "long line boats" for the long lines of baited hooks they feed to the bottom of the ocean, on which the halibut bite, and then are hauled in over the side. The owner was a short German man, Helmut, who had been in the fishing business for years. For the first couple of weeks, Chuck and I helped the skipper ready his boat for the 2,000-mile trip north, to Kodiak Island, Alaska.

The trip up the Inside Passage included some of the most beautiful views I had ever seen. Majestic mountains and dark blue-green water — the colors and views are some of God's best creations. Crewing the ship from Seattle to Alaska did not feel like work. It was spectacular, more than anyone could ever imagine, simply beyond words.

The further north we traveled, the more common it was to see wildlife. One afternoon, as we were making our way through a fairly narrow passage, on the starboard shore was a bald eagle, standing on the beach on one leg, the other leg holding a large crab in its talons. The regal eagle deigned to look at us motoring past him, then continued to take bites out of the crab — much as you and I would take a bite from an apple. It may have been mildly curious or annoyed by us — to me, it was beautiful.

After days of travel with a few stops along the way, traveling through smooth and rough waters, and then three days straight across the open sea of the Gulf of Alaska, we arrived at Kodiak Island. We tied off the boat at the commercial fishing dock our captain used.

On the morning of Opening Day of the Fishing Season, we had everything ready to go. Actually, I kept thinking the skipper should have been showing us what we were supposed to do during the actual fishing part, maybe let us practice a bit. He had told us stories about crew getting their hands hooked by the long line and being dragged to the bottom of the ocean. In fact, there was a knife by the stern to use if someone got hooked and needed to cut themselves loose, to prevent themselves from going overboard. Even under good conditions, it was dangerous work. I hoped we'd get some practice in.

Helmut came out to talk to us, saying there was *"weather coming"*; he didn't know if we should go fishing that day. He looked at us and asked, "What do you think we should do?"

Chuck and I looked at each other, then replied, "We have no idea." We suggested maybe there are other experts he could ask. In hindsight, it should have been a warning indicator that most of the other boats were not getting ready to go fishing that day.

Helmut shrugged and said, "Let's go fishing" — so we did. We headed out to the fishing grounds. Setting of the lines went pretty smoothly. One would cut and bait hooks, the other would clip the baited hooks to the long line, which had an anchor at the end that began to draw the line, baits and hooks to the bottom of the ocean. With anchors on both ends of each line — and we laid out a lot of lines — and a colored float marking each set, we were fishing.

We were off Kodiak Island but we could not see land. At first, the weather was okay, but then it started to change. Within an hour, the ocean waves had developed a random chop, bouncing the boat pretty good. Then, it turned fast.

We were just starting to collect the lines and bring in the gear and any fish we had caught. Helmut was piloting the boat from an outside location while also bringing in gear from the side of the boat. There was a variety of fish, and even a few halibut, which was the goal. However, by now the weather was very serious, and the ocean condition was following into danger as well.

You've probably seen the movies where the waves are so big that the passengers can easily lose sight of any boat nearby. Those swells are bad, but when the wind is high, the swells start to break and double-chop. It is not a good idea to be out in the ocean with waves

breaking over the boat that are larger than the boat.
We were not in a large boat.

I am not sure how we stayed afloat for the next few
hours. It was a full-on assault by ocean waves, wind,
rain — and us trying to get the gear in, and still be able
to head back to harbor. The skipper became so
concerned we could take a rogue wave and be
capsized, we almost abandoned the gear. He had us
get out the survival suits from the bow storage and keep
them nearby.

By the time Helmut and I were hauling the last line,
Chuck was flat on the deck, so seasick he could not
stand or work. Green sea waves were breaking over
the bow, with enough force to push all of us around
where we were standing — or trying to stand.

The storm grew in intensity. Maybe the skipper
panicked a bit because he started yelling at us in
German, which did not lend a sense of calm or
confidence at the moment. Neither Chuck nor I spoke
German; we did not understand his directions. Loose
fish were flopping all over the deck; Chuck was laying
on the deck, and the skipper was working hard to pilot
the boat through the waves.

I did my best to keep working, helping Chuck make
it back to the cabin floor, then back out on the deck,
just trying to keep the hatches tight and everything as
safe and secure as possible, to enable us to survive the
storm. I'm not sure if we knew how close we came to
losing our lives, or if we were simply too busy trying to
keep from dying, but in all that, I never really felt any
emotion of fear. I knew we were in trouble, but I did
not feel fear.

It was like watching a movie, where I could see everything and understand what was happening, but did not have this fear-based emotion; there was a certain detachment. Clearly, I was not thinking of any Bible verses that talked about people fighting for their lives at sea (see Mark 4), but for years I have tried to understand why I was calm inside with everything raging and wild around me. Was it some type of metaphor of my early life? What was God trying to teach me in all this? Was He establishing Himself in my mortal life, with the awareness of the immortality of Life that I ultimately have with Him?

Years later, when dealing with some adult drama in the work place — the kind that doesn't go away quickly, and takes being alert, and enduring a situation that cannot be solved simply or like most problems — that's when I ran across a Scripture that captured the emotion of that ferocious day at sea:

"Do not fear, for I am with you; do not anxiously look about, for I am your God."
Isaiah 41:10

God was with me. Fear has no place when God was standing with me. God is always teaching us. We often think the learning of a lesson is going to occur or happen right after the lesson; sometimes He teaches us, and much later explains it. He weaves events and meanings together in a unique way, just for us.

In our life story — with God as the ultimate Author, and for reasons we won't always understand — sometimes He brings the understanding and insight years later. In God's timing, He connects some of the earlier dots — those which we only partially connect — to show us more of the relevant picture. Faith is realizing the things we understand are mixed with things we don't understand, and trusting that God — Who sees all of these things in the wholeness of our lives — will reveal it to us in the right time. He is God of our whole lives — from the beginning, through the present, middle, all the way to the time ahead.

After 24 hours straight of fighting the ocean, as we neared Kodiak Island, the skipper looked at me and said, "We should not have gone fishing." He commended me for the good job I did out there, but he needed to take Chuck back because he couldn't work with seasickness; he needed to get another crewman.

I could have stayed and worked on that boat. Chuck and I had wanted an adventure, but it was not a career choice. I didn't want to leave Chuck alone on Kodiak Island, but even more, I didn't want to stay on the boat because I was not sure about the skipper. Maybe he was not wise to take a "green" crew out fishing, but it was — pardon the pun — even fishier that his was the only boat willing to go out in that weather. When we got to the dock, both Chuck and I got off the boat and left; the skipper picked up a couple of other crew, likely men who were hungry, unemployed and looking for work.

I have a great deal of respect for those who choose to make their living in commercial fishing. It is hard and dangerous work; it tests a person to their core. No matter how advanced a boat and its equipment, the ocean can and will always have the upper hand — it teaches people to be humble and respectful of a power greater than themselves. That's an important Life Lesson for all of us.

We live in the Pacific Northwest; there is still an industry connected to the waters around Alaska. It has been interesting, later in life, to see some reality-based TV programs about the adventures of deep-sea fishing and crab boats. My hat is off to them.

From the Sea to the Beach

Once off the fishing boat on Kodiak Island, we walked around the Island for hours, trying to find a place to sleep; we had been up all night. After hours of walking — asking folks, not finding much — we were directed by some locals to a place a little ways out of town. It was the home of a very old woman named Minnie, who was known to open her house to strangers on the Island.

We knocked on her door, told Minnie our story, and she said, "You are welcome to sleep in the basement." It was very basic: we each had a sleeping bag on a concrete floor, but it was dry — and not moving, like ocean water — and was very much appreciated. Minnie had about 200 parakeets in her house ... and the two of us were the bird brains in her basement.

The next day, we set about the Island, trying to find jobs. I quickly found a job at an auto shop. My high school interests and experiences with cars, the work I had done in various shops, had given me enough basic experience that I could be useful. Chuck was still deciding which way to go.

It's said there are a few really key decision points in a person's life, times when we have great clarity about ourselves and our lives. For me, one of those came in the back of Minnie's house, where her property looked out over the ocean. There was a fallen tree, and I sat down there on that log, looking out at the ocean.

I thought about all the things that had gone on in my life, right or wrong, over the years. I could have become angry — I had reasons to be — and could continue for the rest of my life with a chip on my shoulder and an attitude to just fight the world. Or, I could become someone, and do something that would be constructive, that would make the world a better place. Mabel Thompson's challenge came to me again: *"Do something important with your life, Nick!"* I knew that would not happen there on Kodiak Island.

Chuck and I flew back to Seattle.

Sometimes God leads us into the wilderness … sometimes we make the choice to go into the wilderness. But even in the wilderness, God will find us … and lead us.

Chapter 17: **SPIDER-WOMAN**

After the Alaska fishing adventure, Chuck and I went different ways for about a year. He got a job near Seattle; I did a variety of jobs living in different parts of Washington State. The next several months probably did not look very productive for those people who had held aspirations for me to play Football at higher levels — but it was productive for me as a person, to find myself apart from the identity and expectations that others had for me, and for the life that I once thought I wanted.

This time also allowed me to help Mom again. She was struggling with my brother Sam, who had a mental health challenge, and was living in a way that put himself and others at risk. Mom — like many mothers — viewed Sam through loving eyes, and was providing food, shelter, clothing, money, and making herself open to his random comings and goings. What Sam really needed was to face his problems and deal with them. He had seen a doctor and was given a prescription for a particular medicine that would enable him to function safely around people. But Sam was not taking the medication, and it was only a matter of time before he could take someone's life, or his own, by his unsafe actions.

I helped Mom do research with mental health professionals, so she could understand the law, to know what help was available for someone in Sam's condition, and do what we could do to require him to get help. Under the laws in place then, the only way he could be forced to get help was if he presented a danger to himself or others. In order to prove he presented this type of threat, there had to be some "other" who could make this statement to the mental health authorities.

Sam came to Mom's house and, based on his behavior, he pulled a knife on me. At that point, I was able to make the statement to the authorities that he had threatened my life; this caused his involuntary commitment for treatment. A judge then required him, by law, to take his medication or be legally picked up and locked up.

My point here is that often we are looking at and trying to make sense of how things are about us in life, when in reality, many times it is about how we are part of someone else's story — and we need to set down our plans and interests, and simply be available, to be there, for others. I was there for Mom, and — in its own way — for Sam as well, getting him the help he needed.

On My Own

Eventually, Chuck and I ended in the same place again, this time in Renton, which is near Seattle. We were renting an apartment and working for the same large company. The money was good, and we were both driving nice cars; we were in our early 20s, with plenty of social opportunities.

I wasn't into the party scene, and — other than work, and going to night school part-time in the evenings to keep up with my college education — I was playing my guitar and writing songs. I went to the gym to keep in shape, and was still sorting out that big question: *"What do I want to do with my life? What is important enough to spend my whole life doing it?"*

A good portion of my life so far had been having the people I trusted — mostly my family, for one reason or another — not being there for me. It had always been a weird dynamic that, as soon as I would start to depend on someone, something would happen and things would fall apart. There were no easy answers.

Chuck and I were best friends; we went all the way back to middle school, and had many experiences together. I trust him; he was closer to me than my family. Sharing an apartment was safe.

One day I came home from work, and was getting ready to drive to the gym, to work out. Chuck was dating a young woman I'll call "Spider-Woman" (I prefer to not use her real name); I didn't trust her because, in my opinion, she was luring Chuck into things that were not good for him. I tried to warn him about what I saw in her, but she had a power over him which I suspect came from an intimate place to which he was drawn.

As I walked through the apartment, Spider-Woman offered me a brownie; she had just baked them. Chuck was standing in the kitchen with her. I took a brownie and ate it, then ate another. I did not detect the marijuana that she had baked into the brownies.

I was about to go to my car when I started to feel awkward. I had never been "high" before, had no point of reference. Now under the influence of a drug, I began to panic, thinking I was losing my mind. Chuck could see my strongly negative reaction unfolding, and tried to tell me what had happened, "It's just the pot in the brownies, man. You'll be fine."

From terror and paranoia, I went to anger, feeling violated by my trusted friend. Of all the people in my life, Chuck knew most of my story, and how opposed I was to any drugs, based on my crazy family life. He didn't know everything — like the abuse I had endured, or some of the things I had dealt with for Mom — but I thought I could trust him, that I was safe around him! Yet, he followed Spider-Woman into her web, and brought me into it as well.

Those who use marijuana, you are probably laughing at me about now. You're thinking, *"What's the big deal?"* I am embarrassed to say it, but I live in a state that has just legalized marijuana! As you're reading this, you're probably thinking, *"You should have just chilled and gone with it,"* right?

I'm not going to comment about marijuana or judge anyone who partakes of it, or any other substances that are used for various reasons. Each person makes their choices in these things. If that is your thing, perhaps it should be done within proper boundaries. I'm not an expert in this area, but it was not my choice to use drugs. I was betrayed by someone I trusted. That kind of betrayal only happens between people; it seems the closer we are to someone, the more important they become to us, the harder it is to experience.

Chuck was devastated by my response. He did not know or anticipate that I would feel that badly about it. Spider-Woman was gone after that happened. That friendship has now been mended. He was young too, and he is still a dear friend!

Changing Gears

Soon after this incident, I decided to leave my job — even with the financial security it provided — and go back to school full-time. This time, I was doing it for the education component, for the opportunity to use my mind and strengthen my inner self in some meaningful way. This time I was ready to use the Football scholarship as the means to help pay for school, but not as my one and only goal in life. This time, Football was no longer a "god" I would serve, but rather a bus to get me to my career.

During these years, I also did different jobs and had different living situations. I learned many things I would not have learned in school, including more about myself, and what it means to survive in a most basic way. I was beginning to understand what I did **not** want to do with my life; winnowing out those options was an important lesson. I learned the value of people, places and things — and the lack of value or limits on the same. The most significant change was taking place inside: I was finding that I liked myself again for who I was as a person who relied only on God. *"Pressing in to God"* was having a positive impact on me.

> *I press on toward the goal for the prize of the upward call of God in Christ Jesus.*
> **Philippians 3:14**

One of the most precious moments during this era was when I volunteered to visit old folks in a nearby retirement home. I connected with a man in his 90s; I'll call him "Alex." He had outlived nearly all of his relatives and friends. I would visit Alex and listen to him telling stories about his life. Sometimes he asked me about my life. Often he wanted to pray, so we did. It was beneficial for me to park the busy pace of my 20-something lifestyle and just see him, connect with him; this was touching and mending a place in my heart that resonated with that place where I felt God inside of me. It wasn't about how fast I could run, or how strong I was, or what kind of car I drove, or really anything external — it was all internal ... and it was healing.

I felt I was adding value to another person's life, by offering him something from inside of me, something close to that heart-and-soul place. I was still not sure what my life career would be, but I was beginning to know it would need the component of helping others, making a positive difference in the lives of others. Maybe it had overtones of Mabel Thompson's long-ago encouragement: *"Do something important with your life."*

"Deaths" In Life

Chuck and I went our separate ways. We kept in touch a little over the years. I visited with his mother before she passed away as she had always been there for me while I was growing up. Still, for many years my friendship with Chuck was different after the brownie experience.

"Death" can happen in our lives and it's not always about our physical bodies. Relationships can die this way. Sometimes I worry that I may have killed a friendship or lost the esteem of a work colleague because of my actions, words or responses. There have been many times when I have needed to surrender my "dead or dying" relationships to God, asking for His help and forgiveness for what I may have done wrong.

Are lost relationships part of Life? Do we break away from others out of a sense of self-survival? Is this just the way of humanity? Are all human relationships transactional, in that we trade each other for something else; and then — when the trading is over and the outcome is not in our favor — do we just close out that account? Does God lead us in different directions — perhaps bringing other people in and out of our lives — for His own reasons?

These are all important questions ... and I was seeking the answers.

Chapter 18: **THE HIGHLANDS**

I am never sure of the timing of things, but I know that God speaks to us when our hearts are really open. God will humble us and cause us to slow down enough to hear Him. This happened with me.

It was right around the unfortunate incident with the Spider-Woman and the harm done to my friendship. Even before I opted out of living at that apartment and deciding what was next in my life, God began to intervene. I had already been invited by a Christian coach to play Football at a different college; my scholarship could be reinstated as a talent award. This college had a Football program that stood for different values than the school I had left. It was easy to reconnect with this coach and make the arrangements to re-enroll in college and play Football again. I was a very different person now.

A Vision in the Daytime

One day, I had taken a reflective walk, finding myself outside a high school in the Renton highlands. There was a large play field behind a high school near where that apartment was located. It was later in the afternoon, but the sun was still visible. There was a scattering of clouds in the blue sky. I was walking and praying, sharing my heart with God. I laid it all open to Him, and was willing to relax in His presence, not expecting anything but open to whatever He placed in my heart. It was a very personal, intimate time in my heart with God.

I was quiet; my eyes were closed; it was a sacred moment. Then I opened my eyes, and could not at first believe what I was seeing! This was not a dream at night — **it was a waking vision.** In the sky I could see a very large screen, spreading miles wide. It was almost like the old drive-in movies, but the images were being shown on the clouds and across the sky. The images were not fuzzy or blurred; they were very clear.

I looked around to see if anyone else could see what I was seeing. My eyes were not closed. I was not imagining it. I was fully awake, and I was seeing this happening in the sky just as real as you are reading these words on this page. The brownie fiasco had been many days before; I was, as I am, clear-headed. I was seeing something I had never seen before.

The "Sky Movie" was image after image of people from every era of recorded History. An image would appear, I could clearly see it, and then it would fade, to be replaced by another sky-filling picture. Men, women, children of all ages ... people from all ages in human History. People in some form or worship or prayer. It was a parade of sorts, a slide-show of humanity. I stood there in awe.

When the images stopped, the sun became brighter, then began to split in a cross-shape of light. The clarity of the light made a certain portion of clouds glow; at the same time, other banks of clouds dulled. I remember this clearly: both banks of clouds were at the same distance from the Cross, but only some clouds glowed with Light while others were dull and fading.

Then the interpretation came to me. I wasn't trying to make sense of this waking vision, but God explained it to me anyway. Those people who seek God through Jesus Christ have been — and are — in God's family, in the Light of His Love. Those who have not sought — or do not seek — God through Christ, are not in the Light and they do not know God. The Light divides at the Cross, thus affirming the significance of Jesus in matters of Death and Life Eternal, as established by His life, His death, and His resurrection. Those who call on His Name come into the Light … and those who do not, are not in the Light. It is that simple for us.

As the warmth of the sun bathed my body and the Light from the sky surrounded me, I knew in that moment that I was being held exactly where I needed to be. I was still in God's hands, still on His path regardless of what I has suffered from others, and the wilderness where I found myself could not keep me from the heart of God.

My Father God embraced me that afternoon. He was in my life, and I was moving towards His will for me.

Purpose and Meaning

After leaving the first college, taking time to travel, work, live, and just experience life apart from Football — and now, finding contentment spending time with God in His Light — I was certain and happy to return to school. To a different college, a different Football program … and as a different person.

I was more mature; it felt good to be heading into a situation where I could use my mind and heart, and not just be working as I had before. There's nothing wrong with a labor-type job; work is a good thing. But the inner tugging and desire to make a difference in some special way was focusing; I could sense that, this time, it was going to happen.

At some point in one's college experience — usually after the first two years of general university credits are met — you have to declare a Major. I pondered and reflected on what career-path had held the most meaning and purpose in my life, up to that point. God had used teachers and coaches to help shape me — I wanted to use that same gift to help shape others. I knew I wanted to become a teacher and coach. This choice was deep and meaningful to me because of those teachers and coaches who had reached into my life and made a positive difference for me. I knew I was on the right path: **Education.**

The college years passed quickly. This time I used Football like a vehicle that helped transport me through school. I was motivated to do well in my classes. I had a great student teaching and coaching placement in my last year. In fact, I opted to not play Football in my last year of eligibility so I could have more time to focus on my student teaching and coaching placement. That experience — and the contacts I made, as well as the job I had done — earned me three different job offers for after graduation, for the next autumn cycle. I graduated with Bachelor of Arts in Education degree.

In the fall of 1984, I took a position teaching Social Studies at Peninsula High School, and coaching for both Football and Baseball. I learned later that I was one of 134 applicants for this particular job. God wanted me there, for sure. I continued college classes in the evenings and on some weekends, working toward a Master's degree, and to earn certification as a school principal. I was effective in the classroom and as a coach, and was encouraged to pursue the principal's credentials as part of an advanced degree. I liked the challenge, regardless of the assignment; all the work added value to the school, and helped students and adults alike.

It was all good, and I have always known it was the right work for me. I truly enjoyed teaching and coaching.

Walking In the Light

One day, I was settling in my fourth period U.S. History class, when the bell rang to start the period; it was right after lunch. There was a test planned that day, and it would take the students most of the class time to complete it. All the students were present in class — except for "Dana," who was one of the better students. Dana was always on top of her work, a really nice person, well liked by her peers.

As I began to give test directions to the students, out of the corner of my eye I saw Dana standing outside the door. She was just in view of the door's glass window; I could see she was crying. I went over and opened the door; before I could speak, she blurted, "Mr. B, I don't know what to do! I need to make a decision, and I don't know what to do."

She was weeping hard, not in any condition to take a U.S. History test; I quietly suggested she should go see the school counselor. I knew well enough that Dana needed more than I could give right then, as I had 32 other students waiting for me. Dana nodded, and left for the counselor's office; I turned back to the students, doing my best to minimize Dana's absence ... and the social "high drama" so common for high school students.

The next day, I saw the counselor and asked about Dana. Quietly, she revealed that Dana was trying to decide if she should take her own life, or not; she had just broken up with her boyfriend, and was devastated. The counselor did an "intervention," and got her parents involved. It was difficult to process but, frankly, not that unusual in any high school.

A few days later, Dana came back to class. She was embarrassed, and thanked me for sending her to the counselor; however, she was more worried about making up assignments, as though she had been out with a cold or something minor. I thanked her for trusting me enough to come by my room.

What always struck me about that situation was the extent to which Dana was so casual, so matter-of-fact in saying she had to make "a decision" — it was a **very serious** decision she was contemplating! I'm grateful she chose life over suicide. This incident also made me appreciate the extent to which so much of public schooling is not only about subject matter or course work, but rather, real connections with young people.

"David" was another student of mine; he was in my third-period World History class. He was one of those students who always wore mostly-black clothes, black leather boots, had bits of metal here and there on his jacket. His work folder, when he brought it to class, was scribbled and labeled with signs and slogans, mostly of heavy-metal rock bands.

David kept to himself; honestly, I think most of the students were afraid of him — they gave him plenty of space. They had heard — and likely amplified the stories — of his activities away from school, including many tales that had him involved in illegal and/or unsafe activities. The combination of his forbidding appearance, the vivid stories, and the general mystique he carried also impacted many of the adults and teachers who interacted with him. At times, even the teachers would comment negatively in the lunch room about David, and I wondered if they were talking about the same person I knew! In my class, David was attentive, but quiet.

My difficult childhood and challenging formative years were kind of a preparation for my years in public education. While growing up, I had been around guys like David in a number of different situations. We're told: *"Don't judge a book by its cover"* — it's likely the "real David" was nothing like the reviews that circulated about him anyway. I gave David the same treatment as I did all the other students; he had to follow the same expectations, participate in the same assignments, and be subjected to the same good-natured teasing I did with all the other students. That was my way to make students feel valued. Students learned … but we also had fun, and we liked each other.

One day, the vice principal came to my classroom and asked, "Why are you marking David as 'present'?"

I replied, "Well, because David is coming to class." The vice principal was a good person, and I was not trying to be sassy, but reporting his attendance in my class was the only thing to say.

He looked puzzled, then said, "David has not been attending any of his other classes. We are about to drop him from the school enrollment for non-attendance." I was floored. Then he added, "The deputy sheriff has been here, looking for David."

"I don't know anything at all about this," I said. "I only know that David has been coming to my class, and he's doing a good job." Shrugging, the vice principal left.

The next day, David came to class, as normal. Shortly after, the vice principal and the deputy sheriff came to the door, and asked to see him. They took him away. I never saw him again.

A few days later, I asked the vice principal about David. He answered, "He has been in and out of foster homes. Now, at almost age 18, he is too old to be placed in another foster home. We learned that he left his last foster home and was living under the bridge at the Purdy Spit, near the school." I was stunned. "David has been burglarizing houses to get money to eat, staying just one step ahead of the law."

I finally asked, "So why has David still been coming to my third-period class?"

The vice principal replied, "When I asked him that same question, David replied, *'It was the only place I felt normal and welcome.'*"

High school teachers are perhaps viewed by some as not supposed to tear-up or care that much about any one student, because they have so many students.

Nevertheless, most of the teachers I know care very deeply about their students — and it breaks their hearts to hear about the struggles in life that some young students have to deal with. I "understood" David and felt compassion for him. I didn't know what would happen to him. I was glad I had been his teacher, even if only for awhile. Perhaps in those moments in my class, he would see something that would help him later in life.

We can often make a difference in someone's life, but don't appreciate the significance at the time. I was now doing for other students what certain teachers and coaches had done for me.

There are thousands of students and their stories I could write; perhaps more can be told in a "later" book. But I share these examples of the importance we, as Christians, have to be Lights in the world, exactly as God calls us:

No one lights a lamp and hides it in a clay jar or puts it under a bed. Instead, they put it on a stand so that those who come in, can see the Light.

Luke 8:16

Really, in any setting or any work, by the way we interact, we can be Lights that attract people to the love of God. Even the scruffy outcasts — in fact, perhaps even more because they may appear "lesser" in the world's eyes ... and perhaps that puts them closer to our Father's heart.

Chapter 19: **PUBLIC VERSUS PRIVATE — OR IS IT?**

Having worked in public schools for 32 years, I know there are many different opinions about what is "best": public versus private, home schooling, private tutoring, etc. **This isn't that book either.** What I want to impart here are a couple of basic truths, and leave the rest to you.

There are really effective teachers in all schools … and some who need improvement. A student needs to be successful academically, socially, emotionally, and more. If a student is struggling in any school setting, it doesn't always mean that the parent should change the school. So many times, if the parent meets with the correct school staff to better understand the student's unique situation, it can result in changing or modifications of **the placement,** even within the same school or system.

It's Placement!

I have counseled parents whose student was doing okay academically, but just not comfortable in the social structure of the school. I have seen students who did great socially, but were not turning the wheel academically. In some instances, they could do the academic work but didn't want to; so we needed to connect them to something that would show them — in their terms — the value of a good education. The fact is: **not all students are created equally** … just as all people are unique individuals.

I have seen students who had a sibling competing with them in the same social pool; we endeavored to help each find their own peer group so they didn't splash (or drown) each other socially. Another time I met with a parent who was convinced her kid could do better with home-schooling. She expected me to debate her, to keep her children in the public schools — instead, I helped her get connected to home-schooling resources, and said that if any time she wanted to bring them back to public school, they were always welcome. When her kids hit middle school, she brought them back to our public schools. She admitted home-schooling was really hard, and she could not keep up with the advanced curriculum as well.

I met another parent whose student had been off in a private school until eighth grade, and was having a hard time transitioning into the public school. We worked with the school counselor to help her meet and make some friends in the high school.

There are so many more examples, but there just isn't space in this book to share them all! Trust me in this, please: **it ought not be a debate about the "school" — rather, it should be a focus on what needs to be happening for EACH student** [21] **to be successful in that school.**

The Value of Light

Christians need to be Lights in the world! Our society needs Christian parents to be active in schools, adding value, not separating from others. We don't help others in the real world if we live in a greenhouse

---

[21] See 1st Corinthians 12:18-30

or fence ourselves off socially. [22] We don't help the rest of the world who are desperately looking for Light, which is a reflection of God's love in and through us — but there will be no Light if we hide or remove ourselves from the rest of the world. And yes, there are people in the world who are not Christians and may have students in the same schools our kids attend. We can, and should, respect them, and treat them with dignity and respect. If we are not Lights for God in this world, we are inadvertently adding to the darkness.

We've heard this a thousand times: *"Christians need to be **in** the world, just not **of** the world."*

*[Jesus prayed to His Father]: "I have given them Your Word, and the world has hated them, **for they are not of the world any more than I am of the world. My prayer is not that You take them out of the world but that You protect them from the Evil One. They are not of the world, even as I am not of it.** Sanctify them by the truth; Your Word is truth. As You have sent Me into the world, I have sent them into the world."*
John 17:14-18; emphasis added (also see John 15:18-19; Romans 12:2)

We are put here to be a living witness of God's love by living around others who hold diverse views. Children learn this from what they see their parents doing. Even precious, innocent children from Christian homes can be Lights in the world, in the public school, because **we have Jesus' promise:** *"My prayer is **not** that You take them out of the world but that You **protect** them from the Evil One"* (John 17:15; emphasis added).

---

[22] See Matthew 5:13-17

I have seen Christian parents become very active with their students, peers, other parents, and their students' schools. Every single day, these parents are teaching Life at home and in church the lessons their young people need to grow in faith, to grow toward God — kids learn from what their parents' model. They help their students learn to process and interpret the real experiences and situations they encounter for life in the real world. Strong Christian parents don't need to try and take over the school curriculum, or pick the teachers, or impose their views on the school.

When the school setting presented objectionable (from my view) issues to my kids, I didn't remove my kids or attack the curriculum — rather, I taught my kids why that issue was something I disagreed with, or viewed differently, and helped them understand and process those issues. We did not avoid them — we faced them, examined them, developed their own core beliefs. **This taught them to actually have stronger core values and better insights, even in my absence.**

What about test scores? People often say that private schools do a better job in educating compared to public schools, and they point to test scores as evidence. What they don't realize is that if one takes students from homes who make that choice (to privately educate), where Education is a high priority, it's also true that they likely have resources, money, values, and time to make achievement important and attainable. Average scores of "these students" will be higher on any test given, as compared to the general public, where many students don't have those same advantages. Thus, using test scores to argue about school quality is more about the socio-economic status of the test-takers.

Personally, I began my elementary education career at a private school; this was my parents' choice. I had excellent teachers, and some who were lacking. Then, when I moved over to public schools, I had excellent teachers, and some who were lacking. What determined my success as a student was very much affected by the quality of my effective teachers and how people responded to what they sensed was a need inside of me. How I responded to them shaped my character and attitudes — and yes, they often spoke into my life or acted on behalf of my father God. **God can (and does) use secular teachers to teach Godly Life principles.**

My two kids, Alisa and Kyle, and my two stepsons, Kael and Jack, were all in public schools. They took regular and advanced classes, based on their interests. They were taught by the teachers assigned to them, and their respective mothers and I did the normal things parents do to support them, their teachers and their schools. If they struggled, we worked with the school on the **placement.**

Placement — that's an important word, and we need to apply it to our children, our students.

Alisa put herself through graduate school, and is now a Veterinarian, practicing near Tacoma, Washington. Kyle, who is deaf, graduated with a degree in Chemical Engineering, and is employed as an Engineer in the State of Maryland. My two amazing stepsons, Kael and Jack, both attend our local public school, and are doing great! More importantly, as parents we have tried to help them all know God in a real and meaningful way. All are good-hearted people who can interact with others in healthy and constructive ways.

I pray that God will give you wisdom as a parent to follow His leading as you assist your children along Life's path.

Chapter 20: **PSALM 22ND (THE ONE BEFORE THE 23RD)**

The 23rd Psalm gets a great deal of attention. It is beautiful and reassuring, all about *"walking in the Valley of the Shadow and fearing not, because God is with us, and how He makes us lie down in green pastures,"* and more. Read it — it is beautiful. So much attention is given to it that I wonder if we haven't created such a spectacular mountain of its beauty that casts an obscuring shadow over what comes before it: the 22nd Psalm. Have Christians created a blind spot over Psalm 22 because of their view of Psalm 23?

If I said the words: *"I have a dream ..."*, most would immediately recognize the powerful opening words of Dr. Martin Luther King's famous speech (August 28, 1963). If I said, *"Four score and seven years ago ..."*, some would recognize President Abraham Lincoln's "Gettysburg Address" (November 19, 1863). The recitation of certain lines would be a short-hand way of drawing our attention to the whole speech, something that is descriptive and meaningful and significant. It's an effective way to communicate many complex, profound concepts. In particular, take note of these phrases, when we're unable to recite the whole speech or literary reference.

The Death of Christ Jesus

From noon until three in the afternoon, darkness came over all the land.   About three in the afternoon, Jesus cried out in a loud voice: "Eli,

Eli, lema sabachthani?" (which means "My God, My God, why have You forsaken Me?").

When some of those standing there heard this, they said, "He's calling Elijah." Immediately one of them ran and got a sponge. He filled it with wine vinegar, put it on a staff, and offered it to Jesus to drink. The rest said, "Now leave Him alone. Let's see if Elijah comes to save Him."

And when Jesus had cried out again in a loud voice, He gave up His Spirit. At that moment, the Curtain of the Temple was torn in two, from top to bottom. The Earth shook, the rocks split, and the tombs broke open. The bodies of many holy people who had died were raised to life. They came out of the tombs after Jesus' resurrection, and went into the Holy City and appeared to many people.

When the centurion and those with him who were guarding Jesus saw the earthquake and all that had happened, they were terrified, and exclaimed, "Surely He was the Son of God!"
Matthew 27:43-54

As shared in the Gospels of Matthew and Mark, the suffering which Jesus endured on the cross had to have been a most painful torture, leading to the demise of His human body. He cried out: *"My God, My God, why have You forsaken Me?"* Clearly, it was painful. And there is no question that He was also feeling the weight of sin of all Mankind, yet He was innocent, without blame. At that moment, Jesus the Son of God was **paying our debt and breaking the hold of Sin on**

Mankind. He was fulfilling what was promised by God to all of us.

When He cried out those specific words, He was also drawing our collective attention to the significance of that exact moment in History what had already been said in Psalm 22. Specifically He drew our attention to the opening line of Psalm 22 **at the exact moment** it was coming alive with Him. He was expressing what had been prophesied in the Old Testament about His death. Those words were written by His ancestor King David, not about himself but about his great-great-great-great (to the 41st generation; about 1,000 years) Grandson.

Consider the message He was trying to convey to Humanity in that very pain-filled moment, where He was fulfilling His mission. What Psalm 22 describes is the entire scene which Jesus was living and dying to teach all of us (hang in with me, because I'm going to include the whole Psalm):

My God, my God, why have You forsaken me? Why are You so far from saving me, so far from my cries of anguish? My God, I cry out by day but You do not answer, by night but I find no rest.

Yet You are enthroned as the Holy One; You are the One Israel praises. In You, our ancestors put their trust; they trusted, and You delivered them. To You they cried out, and were saved; in You they trusted and were not put to shame.

But I am a worm and not a man, scorned by everyone, despised by the people. All who see me mock me; they hurl insults, shaking their heads. "He trusts in the LORD," they say, "let the LORD rescue him. Let Him deliver him, since he delights in Him."

Yet You brought me out of the womb; You made me trust in You, even at my mother's breast. From birth I was cast on You; from my mother's womb You have been my God.

Do not be far from me, for trouble is near and there is no one to help. Many bulls surround me; strong bulls of Bashan encircle me. Roaring lions that tear their prey, open their mouths wide against me.

I am poured out like water, and all my bones are out of joint. My heart has turned to wax; it has melted within me. My mouth is dried up like a pots-herd, and my tongue sticks to the roof of my mouth; You lay me in the dust of death.

Dogs surround me, a pack of villains encircles me; they pierce my hands and my feet. All my bones are on display; people stare and gloat over me. They divide my clothes among them, and cast lots for my garment.

But You, LORD, do not be far from me. You are my strength; come quickly to help me. Deliver me from the sword, my precious life from the power of the dogs. Rescue me from the mouth of the lions; save me from the horns of the wild oxen.

I will declare Your Name to my people; in the assembly, I will praise You. You who fear the LORD, praise Him! All you descendants of Jacob, honor Him! For He has not despised or scorned the suffering of the afflicted one; He has not hidden His face from him but has listened to his cry for help.

From You comes the theme of my praise in the great assembly; before those who fear You, I will fulfill my vows. The poor will eat and be satisfied; those who seek the LORD will praise Him — may your hearts live forever!

All the ends of the Earth will remember and turn to the LORD, and all the families of the nations will bow down before Him, for dominion belongs to the LORD, and He rules over the nations. All the rich of the Earth will feast and worship; all who go down to the dust will kneel before Him — those who cannot keep themselves alive.

Posterity will serve Him; future generations will be told about the LORD. They will proclaim His righteousness, declaring to a people yet unborn: **He has done it!**

Psalm 22:1-31; emphasis added

There's an earlier part of Matthew 27 that bears investigation: *"When [the Roman soldiers] had crucified Jesus, they divided up His clothes by casting lots"* (verse 35). Now read Psalm 22:18: *"They divide My clothes among them, and cast lots for My garment"* (verse 18).

There's also in Psalm 22: *"All who see me, mock me; they hurl insults, shaking their heads. 'He trusts in the LORD,' they say, 'let the LORD rescue him'"* (verses 7-8) — Matthew 27 records: *"Those who passed by hurled insults at Him, shaking their heads and saying, 'You Who are going to destroy the Temple and build it in three days, save Yourself! Come down from the cross, if You are the Son of God!" In the same way, the chief priests, the teachers of the Law, and the elders mocked Him. 'He saved others,' they said, 'but He can't save Himself! ... He trusts in God; let God rescue Him now'"* (verses 39-43).

There were no coincidences taking place on the day Jesus Christ died for our debt of Sin.

Death-Bed Confession

During my time as a superintendent, I needed to get away from the position and "just be me." So I volunteered in my free time to be a "compassionate companion": one who spends time at the hospital with people who are going to die. Often, these were people who didn't have family or loved ones to be with them. Or sometimes we were called to give the family and loved ones a break from the bedside, to regather their strength for the final leg of the journey. Often, the dying person was not awake — at least, not able to have a conversation — and other times, they were fully conscious.

I was called to be with "Charlie," who had only days to live. When I arrived, Charlie was awake, so we visited. He talked about his life, and shared the fears he had facing death. He was worried he would not go to Heaven because, in his own words, he had been "*quite a stinker*" to others in his life, including his own family. His bad behavior was likely why he was dying alone in the hospital.

As we talked, I asked Charlie if he was interested in hearing about Jesus; he was. So I shared the story of God, and the purpose of Jesus' life and death, and the miracle of resurrection. Mostly we talked about the mercy and grace of God to all of us, and that if we ask for it and accept this gift made possible through Jesus, it could change him too. He wanted this, so we prayed for it together.

Then I opened a song on my mobile phone and played it:

You call me out upon the waters / The great unknown, where feet may fail / And there I find You in the mystery / In oceans deep, my faith will stand

And I will call upon Your Name / And keep my eyes above the waves / When oceans rise, my soul will rest in Your embrace / For I am Yours, and You are mine

Your grace abounds in deepest waters / Your sovereign hand will be my guide / Where feet may fail and fear surrounds me / You've never failed, and You won't start now ...

Spirit, lead me where my trust is without borders / Let me walk upon the waters, wherever You could call me / Take me deeper than my feet could ever wander / And

my faith will be made stronger in the presence of my
Savior. [23]

Then I read Psalm 23 to Charlie:

The LORD is my Shepherd, I lack nothing. He
makes me lie down in green pastures, He leads
me beside quiet waters, He refreshed my soul.
He guides me along the right paths for His
Name's sake.

Even though I walk through the darkest valley, I
will fear no evil, for You are with me; Your rod
and Your staff, they comfort me. You prepare a
table before me in the presence of my enemies.
You anoint my head with oil; my cup overflows.

Surely Your goodness and love will follow me all
the days of my life; and I will dwell in the House
of the LORD forever.

Psalm 23:1-6

Every part of the Bible is relevant in Life and in
Death ... and in God's timing, everything happens for a
reason and at just the right time.

On another occasion, I was called to be with an
elderly woman named Dorothy. She was not conscious
when I arrived, but they had told us she could still hear
us. Her hand was trembling. I gently held her hand
and introduced myself. I asked her if she wanted me to
be there. Her hand stopped trembling and she gently
squeezed my hand. So I read to her, prayed with her,

---

[23] *"Oceans (Where Feet May Fail)"* by Joel Houston, Matt Crocker, Salomon
Lighthelm; copyright 2013; published by Capitol CMG Publishing; all rights
reserved; used with permission.

talked to her, and then sang *"Amazing Grace."* She passed away as I was singing. It was a beautiful moment to be part of that passing. I think it was her time to go (and hope it wasn't a result of my singing).

Chapter 21: **COOL DRINKS IN THE DESERT OF LIFE**

It should not be a surprise to anyone who is in God's Family that He blesses us. He loves to bless us! [24]

God's blessings happen in the context of our lives, and often are designed in unique ways just for each of us. Like many things, He may use other people or situations to share something with us. It is always an amazing experience, and one that has just the right emotional tone and substance that is perhaps too profound at times to comprehend. Blessings are not rewards for our behavior — they are God's embraces for His purpose in our lives. Blessings are part of how He shapes, teaches and leads us to become the people He wants us to be on our Eternal Path.

"I Need You ..."

One of my typical routines was to get up about 5:20am and exercise. My afternoon and evening schedules were just too diverse, so to keep a plan, the early morning before work had been the most consistent. Most of the time, I worked out in my garage, combining aerobic, core and strength training. Sometimes I changed it up, and jogged outside with our Black Labrador dog, Stella, so she got some exercise too.

It was funny to watch Stella when she saw it is *"one of **those** days,"* when she joined me in the exercise program — she got very excited! Except when it was

---

[24] See Zephaniah 3:17; also Psalm 18:25-31, 49

really cold outside — then she saw the leash, she sat down by the fire and gave me this *"Really? We are going outside in the cold today?"*

I've always enjoyed being active. Like many people, listening to music is a fun and energizing aspect of a good workout. There are many music preferences, but mine is listening to the local Christian radio station. I like their variety of songs, enjoying most of them, and it is a way to combine exercise with worship and reflection and, at times, prayer.

I had heard the Matt Maher song, *"Lord, I Need You."* It's a soulful, beautiful song where the singer reaches out to God in prayer and worship, with a deep, emotional longing and a sense of appreciation. *"I need You, Lord, I need You …"* the lyrics express this sentiment of a person singing the song to God:

Lord, I come, I confess / Bowing here, I find my rest / Without You, I fall apart / You're the One Who guides my heart

Lord, I need You, oh, I need You / Every hour I need You / My one Defense, my Righteousness / Oh God, how I need You

Where sin runs deep, Your grace is more / Where grace is found, is where You are / And where You are, Lord, I am free / Holiness is Christ in me

So teach my song to rise to You / When temptation comes my way / When I cannot stand, I'll fall on You / Jesus, You're my hope and stay. [25]

This song really touched my heart, and I found myself singing it internally; I sensed it was coming from my heart, directly to God. (That is likely the sign of a good song: when we can identify with it emotionally, when it resonates or relates in some extended way in our lives.) Still, we get busy, Life happens, and a few days later, that particular song faded past me as I went back into my normal routine.

One night about a week later, while sound asleep, I had the most vivid dream. There was no visual image — just the sound of a Voice singing to me: *"I need you, oh how I need you / Every day, I need you ...."* I was very aware it wasn't me singing, that I had not initiated this song to anyone — this was someone singing **to me.** I can't say if it was God the Father, Jesus His Son or the Holy Spirit, and maybe an angel, but clearly, someone from "that side of things" was singing those exact lyrics to me!

Oddly, my first was response was: *"Really? **You** need me?"* How or why could God need me, or anyone? Hearing it was beautiful, certainly, but I felt unworthy. My mind raced, *"This must be some type of mistake!"* Then it gently occurred to me: *"This is all about relationship."*

---

[25] *"Lord, I Need You"* by Matthew G. Maher, Jesse Pryor Reeves, Daniel Carson, Christy Nockels, Kristian Paul Stanfill; copyright 2011 sixstetps Music / Sweater Weather Music / ThankYou Music / Valley of Songs Music / worshiptogethersongs.com / administered by Capitol CMG Publishing; all rights reserved; used with permission.

Yes, we need God — but He wants us, and therein needs us too. Parents: your kids need you ... but don't you also, in some ways, want or need them too, in your relationship? As we grow older and our kids grow older too, they will always be our kids — but they need to begin to establish an adult friendship with us too. A strong connection is two-way. Sure, we can have disagreements with our kids; all relationships have their ups and downs. Through it all, we still need to have some kind of relationship, preferably a friendship, with our children.

God is saying that to us as well. **He wants us, He loves us, He fights for us ... and He died for us, He has won the victory for us, He still lives for us ... and yes, He has a deep and heartfelt longing for us to press in close to Him.** [26] It really is a Family thing! Our greatest blessing from God is that He wants us!

The entrance of Sin into the world broke the relationship between God and His beloved creation, Mankind. Because Sin is still rampant in the world today, God is still calling, *"Where are you? I'm looking for you! I need you ...."*

When my wife Jennifer and I were first dating, I was at her house visiting. She was a single mother of two young boys, was working at an elementary school, was managing the house, and was just a busy person. One day in the midst of all this, I saw her loading groceries into the back of her car. I asked, "What's that for?"

She was bringing food to the school where she worked; it was for poor families. I pretty much knew

---

[26] See Genesis 1:26-27, 3:8-9

right then and there: she was the one God wanted me with — so we got married!

Nine Oh Three

Before becoming my wife, Jen was covering for the principal at the elementary school where she worked; the principal was out of the school that day, so she was acting in that role. The school day ended normally, and the last bus had picked up the remaining kids between 3:15 and 3:30pm.

Jen had just come home after a long day when she got a phone call that one of the students did not show up at home, as expected. This happens every now and then; a student may get off the bus at a friend's house, without previously checking with his or her parents; or a family member may retrieve the student from the bus stop but the message doesn't make it home. These are little human things that happen, and while we know this, there is an immediate intense need to find the missing student.

We have so many safeguards and procedures in place about not releasing students to unauthorized persons, and to deliver students only to authorized bus stops. When a student doesn't show up at home after school, and the parent doesn't know where the student is, the system acts immediately: phone calls to the bus driver to verify where the student was let off the bus … calls to the police … calls to other students who ride that same bus … descriptions of the student are circulated … staff from the school or district go out to drive the route, looking for the student … and even more. There's nothing passive about this important search!

Hours passed, and all these steps were being done, but there was still no word about this student. Jen and I were both working the phones, trying different angles to help locate this student. By 7:45pm, the sense of intensity was now approaching panic, as family and school personnel were desperately working the phones to locate the student. I could tell the emotions — influenced by all the possibilities that could be happening — were taking their toll on Jen, on the student's parents, and all the rest of us as we tried hard to not worry that this young person could have been abducted.

That is a tragic reality in our world. Our young, innocent children are vulnerable. Time passed, many more phone calls and steps were taken, but there was still no sign or word that this student had been found.

The night was cold and clear; it was winter. By 8:30pm, Jen was just beside herself with concern for this student. I was trying to stay calm, but that took considerable effort as the hours passed by. We knew the parents were in pain with worry. We knew law enforcement and others were doing all they could to locate the student.

I was worried too ... yet I had a sense — based on my experiences — that this was going to be fine. But the longer time passed, a sense of dread began to surface for moments in me too.

I tried to stay busy. I took the recycle bin outside. While there, looking up at the clear, dark sky, I just stopped ... and prayed. I was blunt and concise with God, reminding Him of the situation, then pleading

198

with Him from my heart for the safety of the student, and asking Him to comfort the hearts of the parents and all who were in anguish from concerns for this child. Then I was silent.

I felt God say: *"The student is okay, he is safe."*

I asked, "When will we know he is found and okay?"

God said, ***"9:03."*** Quickly I dismissed that as being something my head had invented; it was way too specific to be God's Voice in this moment. Back in the house, I told Jen about the prayer and even sheepishly mentioned "9:03." She was very upset about everything; my encouragement didn't seem to calm her.

At 8:50, we were both at the kitchen counter, having made another round of phone calls. A few moments later, I glanced at the clock on the microwave; it read: *"9:00."* Inwardly, I said, *"Well, God, we have not heard."*

And immediately that same calm Voice said, *"It's not 9:03."* I didn't say anything, but my mind was going back and forth between trusting what I was told — not wanting to be so specific if it wasn't really from God — and sort of wrestling with my faith, belief, trust, etc.

Jen's phone rang. I turned to see her face. She smiled and said, "Found him!" — and the clock on the microwave read "***9:03.***" We were so elated the student was safe and found, that we probably skipped across the clarity of that blessing from God.

The student had gotten off the bus and actually walked from the bus stop to his home. When his parents weren't there, he walked over to a nearby relative's house. He was just doing homework and watching TV. That relative assumed the kid's parents were aware their kid was with him, didn't think to ask if it was okay for him to be at this relative's house. None of these people had cell phones at that time. It had taken nearly 6 hours for the parents to track down their child at this relative's house, and then relay that information to school personnel, law enforcement, and so on.

We all pray for various things in our lives. That situation was the most specific answer to prayer that I can recall, although all of our prayers are answered over time, often in ways we may not always understand. Sometimes it feels like we hear nothing in response; other times it is hard to sort out what God may be saying, mostly from the busyness of our own minds.

God speaks to our hearts. People really need to be able to calm down, be quiet, and be listening.

In the case of the lost student, God alone understood the entire event, and He actually touched many lives, minds and hearts that night. Beyond the blessing of having a child safe, sound and found, which was central to this event — it taught us to more fully appreciate that God is sovereign, fully aware of everything that happens.

That blessing taught us that, while we may have doubts because we are imperfect humans, **there is no valid reason to doubt God.** He is perfect in all things.

Cabo San Lucas

My wife has several close friends who have been there for each other in good times and hard times. All the ladies are married, all the couples are Christians, and all have children who range closely in age.

My wife and her friends love to get together regularly; sometimes they invite their husbands along too. One social experience would be hanging out together, listening to music, maybe playing billiards or board games, and drinking a little bit of alcohol in a safe and appropriate manner. They have fun, they enjoy each other, and they take care of each other.

I am the odd-man-out because I still don't drink alcohol. I am fondly valued as "the designated driver" when the group goes out; I am happy to hold that role, to bring that value to the group. They are all really neat people, and many of our adventures together do not include drinking, so that's not the identifying factor. Still, on occasion, drinking happens.

Another dimension of the "compatible couples with kids" is that everyone works. With parents working and young kids in school, there's a lot of work — managing the home-front, getting kids to sporting events and activities, dealing with work issues. Each family has to work to plan vacation time.

When Jen and I were first together, we planned a vacation with these other couples, going to Cabo San

Lucas, in Mexico, without kids. Jen had been to Cabo before we were married, as had some others, but for the rest of us who had not traveled as much, it was our first time. Just getting all the households organized, making arrangements for kids being safely settled with relatives, for all the couples to be able to reserve that week for the vacation, and all the demands and changes that can suddenly crop up — this was an accomplishment.

The day of departure came … and we all went. The trip was happening! We were all staying at the same resort; one couple owned a time-share, and the rest of us reserved rooms on the hotel-side of the same resort. It was beautiful! Great weather, great food, relaxing by the pools, hearing the sounds and the majesty of the ocean waves crashing on the sandy beach about 50 yards from where we were lounging. We visited a lot, read books, took naps, played cards, and had great conversations about life, kids, jobs, and, yes, matters of faith. I was still relatively new to the group, so it was a relationship-developing experience for me, and them with me.

After a couple of days of "doing absolutely nothing" (and loving it), someone planned a jaunt into town, to visit various places that have music, dancing and, yes, plenty of beer. Some of the clubs and *tabernas* were pretty loud for my generation; "wild," as my wife described them to me. We were still at the resort, and the ladies were putting on their "going-dancing clothes"; I was just hanging out in the room, mostly relaxing and visiting with Chad, Julee's husband.

The truth be told: I was beginning to feel anxious about this trip into town. I had heard stories and —

honestly, had never been comfortable around inebriated people, mostly because they act excessively and loud. I'm more inclined to sit on a beach than go to a bar. Yet, these women are *"24/7, 365 days a year, full-time mothers"* and this was their get-away, a chance to have fun doing something they enjoyed. So, in that context, I was going, and happy to be supportive.

I was also worried that Jen might see me as boring, not a fun guy in this setting (which was really out of my comfort zone). She assured me it would be no big deal, that I needed to relax and just have fun. Her drinking alcohol is only occasional, I don't drink alcohol at all; our relationship works fine for other reasons.

So here I was, sitting in a chair, about 20 minutes from catching a taxi from the resort into town. I was still unsettled, even after Jen assured me not to worry about being the non-drinker in the group. I felt like a life-guard about to become responsible for too many swimmers; it felt like things could get beyond my control. Those were my childhood tapes playing. So I simply prayed, asking God to help me understand my thoughts and feelings, to give me peace and clarity. Then I was quiet, and I listened.

"I will be okay ... I don't need you to protect Me"

That's what I heard God say. *"What?"* God assured me I would have a fun, awesome time with our friends. He was okay with me going; my safety wasn't an issue. Perhaps God knew everyone was going to be fine — more likely He was saying for me not to feel like I was "responsible for everything," that I had to protect Him or His reputation in some way.

I have always been very responsible, perhaps to a fault; it's really hard to truly relax in some situations. Having a strong sense of responsibility works well in my job, but it is difficult to turn that off in non-working settings. God assured me that His safety was not at risk — which one might think obvious — but when my life, and the safety of my loved ones, had been compromised by poor choices and actions by others, especially around the excessive use of alcohol — that sobers a person in a profound way.

I never saw myself as needing to protect God; this was His way of using humor so I would see it for what it was, for me to trust Him and lighten up a bit, to be there — even in a foreign place — to support the social interests of others. In other words: *it wasn't about me!* It didn't need to be about me. God was saying that He is, as always from a greater perspective, still in control … and I didn't have to try to do His job. I was not going to compromise Him by going out with my wife and our friends.

We went … and it was really fun, and funny, to be out with the group. Jen and her friends are so comfortable and relaxed together, they helped others ease up too. They did a good job of embarrassing me on the dance floor — me trying to dance had to be good entertainment. We were socializing in a healthy way; it was refreshing, not foreboding. It was odd that, in that particular social setting, I found more transparency with people; some of our brief conversations were about substance and things that matter. I even found it more authentic how our friends shared their real hearts; not so much shallow chit-chat, but genuine transparency. About the only thing I did not enjoy was the waitresses trying to force "Jello shots" (tiny cups of tequila- or vodka-laced cups of sweet gelatin); but after they realized I was "the boring guy," they found others willing to participate in the merriment.

Everyone made it home safely (I made sure of that). It was a big breakthrough for me to learn how to be up to my elbows *"in the world,"* as it were, yet not be *"of the world"* (see Romans 6:6-14) and be able to relate with people in different settings. There have been many other social experiences with this group of friends and with others, but that first Cabo trip was the true ice-breaker for me. I still don't drink alcohol (don't like the taste), and I'm still the designated driver.

I still smile when I recall what God said to me that night. He assured me it would be okay if I went out with our friends. God has a great sense of humor, and knows exactly what we need and when we need to hear it. He can deliver — in a word or a phrase, or a song — what results in meaningful, lasting, heart-level changes.

Chapter 22: *"LET'S GO RACING!"*

Being physically active has always been central to my enjoyment of life. In addition to organized Sports in school, I enjoyed riding motorcycles, working on cars, snow-skiing, water-skiing, hiking, and other activities. I love going fast, and the feeling of movement that comes with these activities. Still, given that in my middle-agedness, I am into having replacement body parts, I need to manage my activities to work with my body, not against it. Still enjoying those high-intensity activities which I have done, but — with aging — I have had to make lifestyle and activity choices that were challenging.

Serious water-skiing has been a love of mine for years. I was really into it, and spent much time in a water-skiing club, learning to develop my technique on a slalom course behind a tournament-rated ski boat. These are specially-designed boats with tremendous pulling power. Keeping my strength-to-weight ratio optimum helped my skiing, and provided motivation to stay in good shape. I was able to recover from a knee surgery (not related to skiing) and then a two-level fusion of my lower spine (again, not caused by skiing, but certainly aggravated by it). After both surgical procedures, I was able to ski quite close to the level of my former "Personal Best" (PB). I have also had bilateral shoulder and hip replacements, and skied after those too. [My current goal is to ski after cancer treatments.]

Those who understand that Sport, my PB were several full-passes at 34 miles-per-hour and a 32-off rope length. For aging athletes, there is always a marker to try to do something as well as we once did. We know we cannot live and perform at the same level forever, but we are going to give it our best attempt.

There came a point where the wear-and-tear on my body was showing up in problems with my shoulders. When it came the point where I couldn't lift my arm above my head, I knew "the time" had come: I needed to have my left shoulder socket replaced — which would dramatically impact my water-skiing ability for awhile. Since I wasn't fully prepared to reduce my "need for speed" — and with the support of my family — I got a sports car.

When the sports car arrived, I decided to take a performance driving course; this was the start of two years of monthly coaching on a road course track at a racing school, eventually completing the Sports Car Club of America (SCCA) road course racing license. Of course, I couldn't stop with just getting a license — I wanted to race!

It is said, *"Horse-Racing is the Sport of Kings"* — and it is also said that *"motor-sports racing is better left for corporations"* because it is crazy expensive. I wasn't interested in spending my money in buying and maintaining a race-car, and I wasn't sure how deeply I wanted to go into the Sport. My hesitance was not for safety reasons but rather — unless one is paid to drive a race-car, or has a sponsorship to buy, repair and maintain a race-car — all the costs are borne by the person who wants to race the car. This includes any damage to the car, whether your fault or from someone else collecting you in a turn or causing a track accident. When you race at the club level, you may as well sign a blank check before the race and then be prepared to fill in the dollar amount afterwards for whatever level of damage has happened.

My decision was to lease or rent a race-car. Working through the racing school, I was connected to a reputable, reliable firm that rents race-cars. They would deliver the car to the track, and act as crew for the client-drivers, then take the car back when all is completed. They call this "arrive and drive programs," and are not inexpensive but certainly more affordable to try without investing in the full race-car ownership approach. After researching, I signed up for a four-race package that would help me pass the novice level and move to the intermediate level of proficiency.

That's a lot of back-story! So, there has always been a lot of concern about "prayers in school" — and some of that may be justified. But for me, there has always been a good deal of praying when I would get into the race-car … and all of it was justified! I was very competent and well-trained for the races I entered. My fear was not so much my personal safety — I did not want to crunch up the car! The lease covered my use of the car, but if — after the race — the car came back in parts or on the back of a service vehicle, I was responsible from dollar-one for any repairs. I set my budget just enough to cover the rental, entry fees and related travel costs; I could deal with any accidents, but didn't want to have to deal with the costs it would bring.

Clearly I recall sitting in the race-car before my first official race. It was a novice race, with about 20 other cars entered. The officials mostly wanted to ensure everyone knew their flags, followed the rules, and came back with the shiny side of their cars upright.

Most of the turn-workers were volunteers; and there were many safety precautions and inspections done for driver, car, track, emergency vehicles, etc. Honestly, I think people are more at risk driving our personal cars on the freeway, than being strapped into a race-car, relatively speaking.

Visualizing my start while sitting the car, determining the best line to take on the road course, requires way more Math, Science, Physics, and athletic ability in motorsports than I had ever realized … and these were fun and new challenges. Including considerations for high speeds, certain risk elements, the competition factor, surges of adrenalin, and an ever-present awareness that if something goes wrong (as it can and does), it is going to be expensive, I thought, *"What might God be thinking about all this fuss over something so vain, so impractical, so worldly?"* So, in that quiet calm place I knew so well, I asked, "God, what do You think and what do You want to do?"

God replied, *"Let's go racing!"* I'm not kidding! It wasn't like a pep talk — it was more like: *"Nick, this is going to be fun, so let's do this together."* My fears turned to focus as we — God and I — left the Pit area for the start.

I came in third in that, my first race, and then successfully completed three more races that summer. I passed all my novice level races and moved to the next level in my race license program. I met lots of interesting people, had a lot of fun, and learned many things about myself in the process.

I faced and overcame some fears (some which were rational). I happily completed the leased race-car program without having to pay for any repairs or significant damage to the car. (This latter point is rather significant because of the many near-misses that comes with racing. Trust me on this: when a car goes sideways in front of you at 125 MPH, and you have very limited time to react and not much real-estate in which to avoid the car, it not only gets one's attention but reminds you that you're always just inches away from a very expensive moment.)

Speaking in the "royal We" — meaning, *"God and Nick"* — we had gone racing, and lived to tell about it. In reflection, I was glad I did it, and if I had the ability to find sponsors or somehow write it off as a business expense, I would still be racing. However, I'm pretty sure that the public school District would not sponsor my race-car, and I haven't pursued finding sponsors. Now, I just find a good Go-Kart track and give the teens and younger adults a good whooping!

As long as we put God first in everything — and we don't make those "things" to be our "gods — then God is all-in with us in our lives ... and it really is fun "doing life with Him." He gives blessings in ways we cannot imagine. Each day is an adventure with Him.

In the Bible there are many references to *"the heart"* (see 1st Samuel 16:7; Psalm 19:14, 20:4, 119:10; Proverbs 3:1-4, 27:19; Jeremiah 17:9-10, 29:13; Mark 11:23; 1st Peter 3:3-4; and more). The heart is the storehouse of our souls, the place in each person that is most holy and precious of all. When Jesus was referencing His purpose on Earth, He reinforced the importance of the heart for His mission; He quoted from the Prophet Isaiah:

The Spirit of the Sovereign LORD is upon Me, because the LORD has anointed me to proclaim Good News to the poor. He has sent Me to bind up the broken-hearted, to proclaim freedom for the captives, and release from darkness for the prisoners.

Isaiah 61:1

"Anointed" means *"has placed it on My heart"* or *"given Me the assignment."* Also remember that the word for *"prisoners,"* in original Hebrew, means *"blind."* Therefore, *"releasing prisoners from blindness"* means *"opening their eyes with My light, so they can see."* That blindness is the status of all of us who walk in the world and do not see through the eyes of our hearts. We don't see through the eyes of our hearts because we are all broken-hearted by the events of our lives, from young to old. Therefore, Jesus is saying, **"God has entrusted Me with the responsibility to bring Light to the eyes of those who are lost in darkness."** Jesus desires to heal our broken hearts.

Further, Isaiah 61 says we are *"captives"* — captured by Sin, sentenced to Death — until Jesus sets us free because of His death on the cross in payment for our sins, and His resurrection from Death as the Source of our Life!

The Spirit of God was in Jesus. He was sent to all of us, *"the poor,"* because worldly wealth means nothing in matters of our hearts, our souls and our Eternity; we are all desperately in need of God's *"Good News."* Does this resonate with you?

Let's be honest. Let's keep it real. There are significant impacts on our hearts from the wounds inflicted by others. We can hardly watch the News or hear accounts of horrible things happening to people; and then we have our own stories of injustice, neglect, cruelty. People who walk in the darkness step on each other, and that causes pain. It's not until we get a glimpse of Light that we can begin to realize how lost we are, so many miles from what really matters. The Christian life is not about "being an optimist," not about "making lemonade out of lemons" — it's about seeing Light.

Directions to the Destination

When I was about 14, I would ride my motorcycle along the dirt road of a large irrigation canal that ran the length of my home-town, for miles in each direction. From our house, I was able to use alleys, coast across the paved road, and make my way on the canal road, all the way out to the veterinary clinic where I had a job on weekends. My work was to clean out the animal kennels, feed the dogs and cats when the clinic was closed. Once I got locked in an outside kennel with three large puppies. They were very happy to have my company, but it took me an hour to figure how to get out. I have many funny memories from those days.

One day, riding back from the clinic, I pulled over when a car filled with men wearing hunting gear flagged me down. They asked for directions to a particular farmer's field. They had been driving along the canal road for many miles, but didn't seem to be finding their destination. I think they were hoping I'd say, "Oh, it's just a little bit further, you're almost there. Turn this way and turn that way, and you'll be there."

I couldn't tell them that. The more I pondered their destination, the more I realized that it did not matter what or where I told them to turn, they couldn't get there **because they were on the wrong road.** Finally I explained that there were many different irrigation systems in the region, and the road they wanted was clear across on the other side, not even accessible by the road they were presently on. More driving on this "wrong road" would only take them farther and farther away from where they wanted to go. There was no set of directions from me that could have picked up their car and placed it where they needed to be.

The hunters had to go all the way back to get across town and find the correct road. If they followed my directions back to the beginning, at least they had a better chance of making it to their destination. They were pretty good about the mix-up; they turned around and headed back toward town. I hope they made it to that farmer's field.

As I rode the rest of the way home, I thought about the significance of people asking for directions when they are so lost, when they are on the wrong road. When we are wandering around in the dark, apart from the Light and direction of God, when we are so far off track that we won't ever reach our destination, we're in trouble. We cannot find our way on that wrong road, not until and unless we get the divine intervention that lifts our souls, opens our eyes, frees us from all those distractions and attractions that lure us further down the wrong road, with promises that always end up empty. Until God gets our hearts right, we are just lost … and more traveling on that wrong road, in that lost condition, simply takes us deeper into and further along the dead-end road.

It doesn't matter what the distraction (or attraction) we select. We seek meaning and purpose in so many ways, in places that are dead-ends — and I mean that both literally and figuratively — in our lives. The people, the place, the things we use to *"find life"* actually blind us to Life in Christ ... **until we find Him.** When God takes first position in our lives, those people, places and things take on a different, more appropriate value and importance and order in our lives. Only God can — should — be God in our lives, the Captain of our hearts and souls. If we place or make any other person, place or thing that "god" — looking to it, honoring it, serving it — we will end up driving for miles on the wrong road, heartbroken at not finding for what we are looking.

Is God in full view in your life ... or is God in a blind spot where you cannot see Him because of all the "lesser gods" that fill your eyes and block your mirrors?

Please: I am not suggesting I have always had this perspective dialed in. In fact, I have made some really hurtful decisions that injured my heart and broken the hearts of others. I have been selfish and not loving to others. I have sought to medicate and entertain myself, like most people, in both acceptable and unacceptable ways, from the world's perspective and from God's perspective. Just like you, I have tried to keep busy, or sought other ways to to medicate myself so I wouldn't have to deal with things.

Thank God for His mercy to forgive us when we fall so short! Thank God for His grace to bless us in spite of ourselves. Just as we should not be proud, thinking we are perfect (based on our thoughts, words and deeds), we should also not condemn ourselves in the poverty of our thoughts, words and deeds because God loves us and sees us as eligible to be redeemed by the love, sacrifice, blood, and life of His Son Jesus! He wants us to take action, to utilize our faith in order to receive His free gift. [27]

For us to stay engaged with "people in the line" of our lives, we have to see this properly. We are not good enough to earn our way or pay our way to Heaven — only Jesus Christ can do that, and He's **willing** to do that in us. And, in spite of the thoughts, words and deeds that actually lead us to Hell, we cannot dwell on our stains — because once we accept salvation through Jesus, those stains are "past," we have been washed clean by the beautiful, cleansing gift of love and grace, given to us as heirs and children of our sovereign God!

> *The Spirit Himself testifies with our spirits that we are God's children. Now if we are children, then we are heirs — heirs of God and co-heirs with Christ — if indeed we share in His sufferings in order that we may also share in His glory.*
> **Romans 8:16-17**

---

[27] See Romans 10:8-13

Each one of us is *"a work in progress."* It helps nobody if we get discouraged when we stumble. When we mess up, understand your motives, and ask God to help you at that place in your heart. Then just pick up the pieces and try to fix whatever you screwed up, especially the parts that impact the lives of others. Learn from it, and keep paddling forward, working to apply what you learned, and to do better as you move further along.

We are born with Free Will — the option, the freedom of choice — and there is significant power in the choices we make over time. We have the power to heal ... or the power to hurt. We have the power to support, encourage, inspire, sustain, endure ... or the power to ravage, discourage, retreat, give up. How we use our free will is a choice, and it is a tool we can use to honor our love and life with God ... or move ourselves for whatever motives in other directions, on the wrong road.

Imagine you are in a River that is moving. The River is Life, and the movement is the sovereign will and direction of God in the Universe. Some things are predestined, but most things (within this flow or context) are subject to us and the choices we make.

Don't get distracted: there **are** major themes which are *"foretold," "ordained"* or *"predestined"* for Mankind. What we're talking about here is that, in the River, we have been made in the likeness of God, and given the power of choice, the free will to use to move around in the current. We can even get off and sit on the bank for a while. We can go with the flow, and hit rocks, gets snagged on hidden things, dunk others (even drown them), or offer a hand to those who are struggling to keep afloat or whatever.

The thing is: **God wants us to reach out to Him in this River, to let *His* motives become *our* motives — and above all else, His motive is to love people!**

Do we seek *"fruit from the Tree of Life"* [28] to strengthen that which remains ... or do we see ourselves as demigods craving *"fruit from the Tree of the Knowledge of Good and Evil"* in our attempts to gain Life?

Yes, it is hard at times. The views of other people can be so harsh. We find ourselves being criticized or judged on one side for not being "good enough" or not conforming to how some say a Christian life should be. We can find ourselves just as distant from those who have rejected God and the beautiful relationship we have with Him, often because of what others have done *"in the name of religion"* or because they are in love with false gods. To be healthy with God in our own lives, we need to take those "opinions of others" and flush them! Live your life and be purely connected to the Love and Light of God, taking it directly to your own heart, and don't let that become distorted by the views of others.

God loves you. He knows you, and He's willing and available to have life with you. It is the best friendship, the best Family, the best of an ultimate and sincere and glorious connection to our Creator. It is the Source of Life in this life and is the Source of Life Eternal.

---

[28] See Genesis 2:15-17

The Garden

Just for a moment, consider how much Jesus Christ, the Son of God, loves you! He was willing to give absolutely everything to reach across the broken relationship between God and His children, and draw us back into God's Family. It was not religious persecution that brought about His death — it was the fulfillment of God's plan to pay our debt and wash us clean from Sin, and the only payment accepted was the life of His Son.

Recently I woke up with this poem singing in my heart:

My Father called to Me, and said,
"What grieves You so, My Son?
You pray and weep in the Garden now,
You are the Chosen One."

"My enemies are meeting,
They are plotting My demise.
My friends asleep beside Me now,
Tears flow from My eyes.
I understand what I must do,
This gift of love so pure.
Spare Me from the pain,
The torture I must endure!
The choice of Sin that caused the Fall
Requires Love's Sacrifice,
And only those who call on You
Will be worthy of the price.
In You I commit My life for salvation of lost souls;
I will Your promise fulfill,
And make what's broken whole."

'Twas then the sun began to rise,
And the Son too from His knee;
And the Gift for all Eternity
He gave for all who see.
The One Who gives life,
Traded our sins for His pain.
He is our breath, our heart and soul,
And now forever reigns.

Jesus paid a tremendous price to cancel our debt of Sin. He did this willingly, He did this lovingly, He did this so sacrificially. It's a free gift He offers to you.

My Prayer For You

"Laying at the feet of Jesus, we reach out to You, dear God. Thank You for knowing us at the deepest level. Thank You for the air we breathe, which fills our lungs ... for the water we drink, that gives us life ... for the rest we find in You, that restores our hearts ... and for the courage we have when filled by Your Spirit, that enables us to show love and make a positive difference in the live of others.

"As we walk and meet others in this world, help us to be the Light of Your eyes and reflect the Love of Your heart. Empower us to bring rain to dry and lifeless deserts, where life is slowly drained out of people. Establish us in Your good will and sense, to show wisdom, life and substance to those who are lost in this over-stimulated amusement park of self-made entertainment. Give us the insight to claim Jesus' power and victory, to overcome and resist

evil that would take us out of Your River. Help us to make good choices, and use our God-given gifts well.

"Keep us close to You and close to each other, as You lead us in our lives with You, and as we represent and bring Your Kingdom to others. In the precious and powerful Name of Jesus Christ, we pray. Amen."

Chapter 23: **WHY WE ARE HERE**

I **used to think there was a special path or life** I was supposed to live, and it meant leaving the life I was living, probably traveling to some foreign land, putting on a simple robe, being poor, and bringing God's love and Words of Life to people far away. I had this idea that's the kind of life we were being called to live.

One day, very deep in prayer, I gave this idea to God, and opened myself to His answer regarding what path and place I should live and walk for Him. I honestly assumed He would tell me to sell everything I owned, put on sandals, and move to some Third-World country — sort of "Mother Teresa like" but with a beard. Don't get me wrong: I have great respect for Mother Teresa and those who actually do take that path. But what God put on my heart was not at all what I anticipated.

He said, *"Nick, the path you are to walk is the same one you are on. It is where you are now, doing what you are doing — just doing it for Me."*

Part of me was a little disappointed because some aspects of my current path have burdens and are not really filled with the glory of a Godly life, at least as much as I wanted it to be. I wanted my path to reflect a strong Christian life, as I defined it, but I was falling short. I thought I was disappointing God, and I wanted to do more for Him, so I asked the question. His response showed me that, in fact, He wants me exactly where I am, and with the very people I am with, some of whom I like and — frankly — some, not so much.

I've always tried to "love God's way" but, truthfully, there are some people I just don't like. Nonetheless, God calls me to love these people, here and now, where they are, and where I am at with them. Part of me rebelled. *"Oh, God, You're saying I'm going to have to 'turn the other cheek'* [29] *and 'give my extra cloak'* [30] *and 'give more than they deserve,' aren't You?"* It didn't work.

He has called me to show grace and mercy, to love in spite of the things or people I don't like. The path He wants me to walk is the one I am on, not some other place (at least, not right now). It's called *"picking up our cross and carrying it daily"* [31] — it happens daily with the lives we are living. If (or when) God wants to change the landscape dramatically, He will.

Our purpose is to live this life, to show love, to accept and embrace the roles He has for us in each time and each phase of our lives. It's not punishment. Once we really give it all to Him, He brings joy back into our hearts in the midst of the day-to-day lives we live, right where we live, and with whom we are living and working — even when it is hard.

Just as there are different roles in life, or work, or in families, there are often really different roles in God's Family. His Kingdom of believers and followers are the windows through which He brings Himself into the world. There is a purpose and reason for this

---

[29] Matthew 5:39; Luke 6:29

[30] Matthew 5:40; Luke 3:11

[31] Matthew 10:38

differentiation of assignments. Clearly, with God as our focus and with love as the unifying spirit of all we do, there are times when we wonder, "Why am I here?"

God has shown you, O mortal, what is good. And what does the LORD require of you? To act justly and to love mercy and to walk humbly with your God.

Micah 6:8

When we show compassion to others when they don't deserve it, we are showing God's grace and mercy, and bringing His love to a lost world.

What we do (INSERT YOUR JOB OR ROLE) isn't as important as **why we do it,** and **how we do it,** and **for whom we do it** — these are conditions or reflections of our hearts. When our hearts are tuned into God's Spirit — the Source and Wellspring of Life [32] comes out in those moments. Yes, God wants us to walk the path of Life with Him — and it is the path that is before us **now,** not one we have to drive or fly somewhere to find.

Many times, we are "striving" (definition: *"straining, using much effort, trying too hard"*) for a new job, or a new house, or obtaining anything new, better, different, etc. There'a place inside us that drives our striving; often humans harness this dynamic or energy to improve our world or upgrade our situation, to obtain a functional benefit. We often believe that achieving those ends will bring meaning and lasting peace in our hearts ... but that is delusional. That inner place really wants and needs one thing: union with

---

[32] See Proverbs 24

God our Creator, the love of our hearts, the meaning of our lives.

Learning *"to be content in all things"* [33] comes from enough life experience to appreciate that all things apart from God do not bring lasting contentment. Often it's when we have tried a lot of these *"other things"* yet end up wanting more, that's when we realize that no amount of sea-water will quench our thirst. These people, places and things can be blessings in our lives if, or when, they come after we are right with God in our hearts. More often, however, we end up making them "gods" in our hearts, resulting in a mouthful of dirt and no lasting or deep satisfaction. [34]

Summation of Life

- I have had success in Sports and received the recognition of many — but it was nothing without having God in my heart and life.

- I have had nice houses, some of which I designed with water-views and access — but they were nothing without having God in my heart and life.

- I have had wonderful relationships and intimate experiences, which one can only dream about — but it was nothing without having God in my heart and life.

- I have traveled to beautiful places, and had food prepared by the finest chefs in the world — but it

[33] Philippians 4:11-13

[34] See Matthew 7:24-27

was nothing without having God in my heart and life.

- I have held my children in my arms, and had moments of laughter and meaning in my family — but those passed by quickly and did not last, compared to God in my heart and life.

- I have held positions of respect, and have been paid well for work which the world honors — but it was nothing without God in my heart and life.

- I have used people and have been used by people; I have trusted and been trusted; I have been loyal and I have been betrayed — but none of that compares with having God in my heart and life.

- I have done well, and I have done poorly; I have experienced every emotion one can have, and most of the experiences that can be packed into one man's life — but these were nothing without God in my heart and life.

The sum of our lives is often determined by looking back and seeing what we accomplished — with our family, with work, with life. When one adds up all these things, they pale in comparison to Eternity. In the long run, the place of grace in our salvation is where we find Life, not in the lives we try to arrange for ourselves along the way.

"The Least of These .."

Jesus Himself told us:

"Truly I tell you, whatever you did for one of the least of these brothers and sisters of Mine, you did for Me."
Matthew 25:40

That's profound.

Most of the time, there is a crush of activities happening in a school District. When I was working in my last District, we had about 20,000 students, plus parents, relatives, community personnel in the mix. Add in nearly 4,000 employees, with a variety of jobs and roles in the system, and ... well, let's just say that while most of the time, 99% of everyone is spot-on in their words and actions, there are clearly times when some people zig rather than zag, and it requires follow-up to put it all back on track.

There's always a mix of dealing with the specific event that happened (or malfunctioned), then learning from the misstep to know how to improve the people or the system to better go forward. Public schools are not just about the academic learning of the students — the adults need to be learning too, in order to maintain our viability with the public, the parents who send us their precious children and their hard-earned money to make it all work.

One rare day as a superintendent, I found myself having a very small time-window of "calm": a point where there were no meetings, no messages, no emails that needed to be answered. It was a few minutes to simply wait for the next thing, either something unplanned that was inevitably going to find me, or something I would initiate to do. I was able to sit for a moment and reflect on how this was my 20th year as a public school superintendent, and my 30th year of working as a teacher and coach, and building District-level Administration positions. I wasn't in those roles for long; but I accomplished a lot while doing them.

With so many years having passed, I wondered how or why God had blessed me to remain so long; the career of a large District school superintendent averages only two or three years in duration. I did not have an answer in that moment, only the lingering questions: *"Why God? Why me? Why in this work for this time?"* I was in a contemplative mood.

Then, my phone rang. I barely answered the phone before I heard the voice of a woman — I'm going to call her "Betty" — the mother of a son who had been disciplined by a school employee for an infraction … and it was not a pleasant voice. Betty was angry, she was caustic; she did not like the way the employee had treated her son and had treated her. Betty was almost abusive in how she spoke about the people in our system with whom she had communicated. She had talked directly to the employee who insulted her son; she had talked with that employee's supervisor; now she was talking to me. She was not happy!

At no point as she shared her complaint about how she had been treated, did she feel she had been heard or felt like the issues she felt were wrongful were going to be addressed. Actually, this was not frequent in our system; most of the time, at the first level of contact or shortly thereafter, a complainant is heard, issues are addressed fairly and respectfully. Maybe the outcome doesn't satisfy the complainant, but effort is made to have reasonable communications.

It is unusual for a complaint like this to work its way up the chain of command. Often there is something unique about the situation when this happens. I suspected that how Betty was communicating would have an impact on anyone with whom she had previously spoken: it was a bit like standing in the face of a hurricane or tornado, with large objects flying towards you!

I gave her as much time as she needed to share her complaint, first about the issue that had happened with her son, then the perceived response of the employee toward her son, then her perceived response of the employee towards herself, then her complaints about talking with two different levels of supervisors. After about 20 minutes of simply listening to her, she paused a bit in the "conversation," which seemed to indicate that she wanted to know if I heard her — and, if so, what was I going to do to address the now-multiple issues she brought. The expedient thing would be to jump into a problem-solving mode, which is actually much too common and easy for me, a trait I have over time learned to hold back.

Instead, my first response: **I wanted to make sure she felt heard.** Calmly, I paraphrased the items she had shared, not just the substance of the issues but how I heard how she felt injured by each of them. About 80% through this reiteration process, I could hear her: she was weeping. As I described her perception, she was weeping with relief and hope, and some of her hurt was washing away.

I then asked Betty if I could investigate more about this situation before sharing what might be my next steps. She agreed. Keep in mind that all of this was taking place over a telephone line, not in person.

I learned she was a person of color … a single parent … whose child was a special needs-student. They had recently moved to this area "to get a fresh start." Their home was just the two of them; they had come to this area to get a new job and were hoping for a better life. Her son had experienced difficulties in his previous school. Her job was their only source of income. She was stressed with typical single-parent challenges, which were even more complicated when dealing with a special-needs youngster.

Betty was struggling with the basic logistics of getting to and from school for her son … her starting a new job … no friends, no relatives in the area to help her. They were alone. The last thing she needed thrown on her plate with drama was a problem with getting her child to and from school, nor did she need to experience being treated with a lack of dignity or respect by one of our staff. Nor, when she asked for help at the higher levels but did not experience it a way that resonated with her, she was undone. And she did her "undoing" through the phone right into my office, loudly and stormily.

After time spent relating with her, and agreeing how challenging it all was for her in her situation, I asked if she was ready and open to hear my thoughts about how best to move forward. With nearly a sigh of relief, Betty said, "Yes, okay. Now what can be done?" She listened as I outlined the specific issues I felt were happening in that situation. I explained the steps I would take to look into each issue. I shared with her when and who would get back to her of each of the identified steps — and then left the phone call because my next actual appointment time had come. As I hung up, it was like talking with a different person; gone was the hurricane — now there was a mother who had hope and knew she had been heard.

After my meeting, I contacted three different staff people, assigning each to look into some aspect of this situation. First I wanted to ensure that the educational placement of her son was correct and appropriately supported. I wanted to investigate the allegations of the employee's interactions with her son and with Betty. I wanted an answer if the special-needs status of her son could open more options within the school transportation challenges. I made contact with the school principal to share with him the initial complaint, and to update him with what I had learned about her and her son so he could keep an eye on things as well.

Within three days, all the follow-up had taken place. One thing uncovered in our investigation was that the employee did cause problems for the son and then for Betty; this resulted in him receiving additional remedial training. We found a special transportation option that was better for Betty and her son. We confirmed that his educational placement, program and support for the student at the school was appropriate and being monitored. All of this was conveyed back to Betty.

I rarely have to take any supervisors "to school" (issue correction) on these things that get past them and eventually come to me. The staff usually feels self-conscious when that happens, and try to figure out what happened before it gets to me. In our regular "base-touching sessions," we review how things were processed, and learn what might have worked better or been more effective. I also learned from my staff how to improve my performance. It is a great team of people, each adding value to the important work of educating our children.

"For Such a Time As This ..." [35]

A few days after talking with Betty, I asked God why He allowed me to stay in this work, at this level, and gave me opportunity. He answered, *"Because you love My people."* The whole interaction and advocacy with Betty and the staff flashed through my mind. God was teaching me that — while it is my job — there could be different ways to handle that situation ... and it could have been a mine-field.

Some people in this world see others as "lesser" — in resources, in status, in education, in social access, in a hundred different ways. We sort and classify and separate ourselves from other people based on differences we see, perceive, create, or assume to be true. Even I did this, I suspect, perhaps in ways I was not aware, regardless of my intentions or motives. Why? I am a Caucasian male, with an advanced education, with a good paying job, who has benefited from privileges earned — but also because of being born in this world with these "credentials." Regardless of my motives (which I thought were good), not everyone has the cards dealt to them in favorable ways,

---

[35] See Proverbs 31:8-9; also Esther 4:13-14

not in the world's eyes and not in the culture's view, especially in this country.

I struggle with the notion of seeing anyone as "higher or lesser" in value, based on physical or "worldly" criteria. This is how many people in the world see and experience other people, and it impacts how they interact with them, how they treat others, the expectations with which they operate, and, most importantly, if or how they show love, respect and dignity. Social class can also impact how people feel about themselves, and how they interact with everyone else.

A wise man once told me: *"Anger is a secondary emotion, there is always another more basic feeling under the anger."* What is that *"other emotion"*? It is **the need to protect ourselves.** Thus, when I met an angry person, rather than react to the anger, I always waited and searched for the more basic emotion, the unspoken reason that was beneath the surface.

When we give our lives and hearts over to Father God, He writes a new code into the program that runs us — or another way to express it is, He gives us new eyes to see, eyes that perceive from our hearts, not our minds ... eyes very much like His — and through these eyes of our hearts, we see and experience people differently. Of course we all still do those customs or traditions or ceremonies that we think are proper, especially when responding to "someone important" ... but there is a new and better way to live.

With God's eyes — choosing to let the eyes of our hearts see — each and every person is important and to be loved, even when they are struggling. Those whom society scorns, those who are pushed away from or looked down upon — they too are loved by God. If we take the time to learn their life story, we would likely see some reasons that caused them to end up where they did. Or perhaps to better understand why they would use their free will to end up somewhere unsafe or unsavory, or even ended up as victims in situations by the hands and choices of others.

Our job is not to judge the value of "others" as "lesser people," nor is it to always judge the circumstances that led them to that place, but rather to remember and act on the fact that they are not lesser in God's eyes, **have the same value as we do in God's heart,** and so to love them in spite of the things that might otherwise cause us to turn away. That is what we are called to do. **Right here, right now: *"Who is in line with you?"***

On our own power, with our own determination as people, I doubt this is possible or sustainable for any length of time, or in any meaningful and significant way. But giving God active access to our hearts, and with His strength working in us — yes, all things are possible, and those mountains can run to the sea!

> *Jesus said, "Everything is possible for one who believes." ... "Have faith in God," Jesus answered. "Truly I tell you, if anyone says to this mountain, 'Go, throw yourself into the sea,' and does not doubt in his heart but believes that what he says will happen, it will be done for them."*
>
> **Mark 9:23, 11:22-23**

I still have days when I wonder about life. I take each day as a gift and opportunity blessed in my life by God, and pray that I can and will do for Him and "the people He loves" (which is everyone) to add value and be constructive and be supportive and be loving in His way. I will keep walking this path and through this door as long as He wants ... and unless or until He opens another Door for me to pass through.

Chapter 24: **PLACING FAITH IN JESUS CHRIST**

Placing our faith in Jesus Christ — not in other people, no matter what — is essential for us to be connected and consistently walking with God in this life. It is so easy to want to find unconditional love in people — there is an inner tugging in our hearts, and we seek to fill this craving and longing with people who are often seeking the same thing. Yet we are not "gods" nor capable of being that for another; and those others cannot be "gods" to us. If we try to make them gods, to fill up the places of our hearts with them, we create a burden which they are not capable of carrying. We often set ourselves up for betrayal and disappointment of such significance that it can cause ruin and heartbreak, and leave us broken down on the side of Life's road.

It is important to ask ourselves: ***"What is my faith based upon?"*** Is our faith based on members of our family? Is it with some friend or person we've known for years? Is it a person of faith, such as our church pastor, or another? Here's a news flash: **If our faith is placed on <u>anyone</u> other than God, we are either in trouble, or about to be.**

Humans are just so inconsistent, so frail, so ambivalent, so needy, so wishy-washy, so human. We can and do have great moments when we can be noble, and loving, and kind, and smart, and capable, and loyal, and dependable ... but we are still human, and humans mess up a lot, often, and sometimes, at the weirdest times in unsettling ways!

People seek to fill their inner drive and longings in a million different ways, but the only lasting way to find fulfillment is with God. Don't expect people to screw up, but don't expect they won't … and when they do, don't make it: *"That's on You, God, You messed up"* — **it is always about human failings and not about God.**

Many people hear about or see someone doing something terrible or unloving, sometimes claiming it's "in the name of god" that they chose to do these awful things. Then the great audience of Humanity sees these atrocities, and come to the conclusion, *"If this is what 'godly' people do, then it must be about their god or something."* They want to put cruelty onto God in *"the name of religion"* — when it's what people are doing, not "god" or God. This is when the real God just shakes His head at all of us and all this, and actually, He waits for us, individually or collectively, to figure it out. God is very patient. [36]

Another human "complaint about God" is because of the many Biblical references to *"the Glory of God."* The misconception is that *"God needs Glory,"* like He has some grasping, ego-driven need. God's Glory — or "His Light" — is more for our benefit, like a lighthouse that ought to attract us to Him, to help keep our ships off the rocks. Our faith is in our confidence in God for the entire journey across the Ocean of Life; throughout our lives, we are being drawn to His Majesty and Glory as our Light. God's bright Glory moves us forward in the darkness and overcomes the misdirection that overtakes so many who are lost, in the dark, and don't even realize they are dying. So many don't realize how

---

[36] See 1st Timothy 2:3-4

lost they are as they strive to find themselves in the wrong places and with the wrong people!

God Honors Faith

In Matthew 8, there'a story about a Roman centurion who had such confidence in Jesus that he did not even need Him to go to his house in order to heal his servant:

> *When Jesus had entered Capernaum, a centurion came to Him, asking for help. "Lord," he said, "my servant lies at home paralyzed, suffering terribly."*
>
> *Jesus said to him, "Shall I come and heal him?"*
>
> *The centurion replied, "Lord, I do not deserve to have You come under my roof.* **But just say the word, and my servant will be healed.** *For I myself am a man under authority, with soldiers under me. I tell this one, 'Go,' and he goes; and that one, 'Come,' and he comes; I say to my servant, 'Do this,' and he does it."*
>
> *When Jesus heard this, He was amazed and said to those following Him, "Truly I tell you, I have not found anyone in Israel with such great faith."* *... Then Jesus said to the centurion, "Go! Let it be done just as you believed it would."* *And his servant was healed at that moment.*
> **Matthew 8:5-10, 13;** emphasis added

Jesus marveled at that level of faith! The centurion's faith was honest, real and present. It didn't take a bunch of formulaic prayers, or dancing around, or politics, or other people *"doing the faith thing"* for him. He simply said, *"Here is my need. My heart is involved as this is someone I care for. In my work, I can give orders and others fulfill them; I can do things for others and they get done. Others follow my lead as they are supposed to do. So now, Lord, if You can and will heal my servant, please just do it by saying the word, and I know it will be done."* That is it.

We all have realities of life and survival in the world. We need to live practically **in** the world, but we don't have to be **of** the world (see John 17) — meaning, we don't have to give our hearts to the world, we would be wise to only give that special part of ourselves to God.

Another place in Matthew's Gospel says:

Do not give dogs what is sacred, do not throw your pearls to pigs. If you do, they may trample them under their feet, and turn and tear you to pieces.

Matthew 7:6

This isn't harsh or fatalistic judgment that *"all people are dogs or pigs,"* but rather it is meant to understand that people inherently are not able to hold or keep in a proper way those very sacred and special parts of our hearts. The treasury of our hearts are best and only safely shared with, and held by God, Who knows us and loves us at this level, unconditionally, at the very core of our beings.

How do we live in the world but not be so drawn into it that we are tempted, seduced, fooled, deceived, and end up missing real life with God (which is our true salvation in this life and leading to Eternity)? The answer to this life-quest is our enduring life of prayer — the life that comes to us from God Himself.

A Place to Pray

When my wife and I stayed with relatives while visiting her father, Roger, in Yakima, Washington. He lived in a small camping trailer in a mobile home park, so when we went to see him, there was more room at his brother Pat's house. Pat and his wife Gale always welcome us when we came. We took the kids as well, so everyone would have more time together.

This trip was only a few weeks since Roger had been diagnosed with advanced lung cancer, and we weren't sure how many more chances the kids would have to see their Grampa. The time between Roger's diagnosis and his passing was just a few months.

[Quick SEGUE (which will make sense later): While we visited in Yakima, I was heading out for an early morning run when I noticed a house nearby was setting up for a yard sale. As I ran past their house, I glanced at their wares, thinking I would visit when I returned from my run. When I came back later, I found a collection of old books; I purchased a book on prayer for 50-cents. Over the next few weeks — and particularly since it was the end of the school year, which is a heavy schedule; plus Jen was helping her Dad with his medical treatments — there wasn't much time to do any personal reading.]

Roger's doctors tried some procedures and some chemo, but shortly he developed an infection that they could not reverse. Jen made the solo trip to Yakima to be with him in the hospital; I remained at home with the boys, supporting their schedules. She remained at his bedside for those days, keeping him company, having good talks. She was also his advocate with doctors and nurses in terms of pain management, and ultimately she dealt with the particulars of his passing and the details that followed.

Roger was a character. Imagine the persona of a "cowboy" and try to transplant that to our era — that was Roger. He lived a very modest, humble existence, did various handyman jobs to make just enough money to get by. The way he lived, he didn't need very much. Roger wasn't much for religion or any faith-based things; he had a passion for horse-races, and could always pick the winners. While he didn't have or want enough money to gamble much on horse races, he would at times give his "picks" to others, who could often cash in on his expertise.

Roger said he had "experienced God" — or so he thought — through many other people who professed to be of that orientation. From his view, there wasn't much to make of it, at least not positively. Like many, he had tossed aside any sense of spirituality or "hope of God," mostly because of the hypocrisy (in his opinion) of what he had seen and experienced from religious people. I suspect he felt that he wasn't good enough, a self-imposed isolation of sorts, one where we would all be accurate if we viewed ourselves without the context of God's grace and salvation.

Each of us lives in a sort of self-imposed prison, often reinforced by other inmates around us, until we are set free by the gift of God's grace through Jesus.

Our freedom from our prison is already paid, but accepting that freedom necessitates getting up and walking out! Only prisoners who understand and claim this — that they are pardoned — can actually get up and get out; otherwise, it is safer and more comfortable to stay in that prison, which is a known habitat, even if bleak.

Before Roger died, Jen and I were talking during one of her breaks from his bedside. She was exhausted. She was emotionally spent from being there for him, while dealing with her own mounting grief as she was literally watching her father die. She tried to take little naps, but clearly was not getting enough sleep, as we all need.

There is a fight to live, a clinging to life, a sense of urgency as most people are brought to their final days. We seek a life-saving answer from medical experts, and we even pray that the outcome would include keeping the person with us longer. Maybe it takes that last fight before we can surrender, but I have often wondered if we are doing it for ourselves or for the person who is dying. It was very tough on Jen.

That day, Jen and I were talking on the phone, and I asked her if she thought her Dad would want to pray with her. She knew he wasn't much for religion, but also that he loved and respected her, and he knew she loved him and was standing by him. He knew she didn't judge him or try to change him, only that she was there for him, no matter what.

Jen asked Roger if he wanted to pray with her. It was a bold and courageous move on Jen's part as she is rather conservative in her expressions of faith (although her actions totally reflect her faith). Still, she had to overcome her hesitance, as well as a fear of how her Dad may react if she reached out to him in the final hours.

Jen asked if he wanted to pray, and Roger answered, "Yes." Together, they prayed. She told him it was okay for him to go, that she would be okay. She took his hand and placed it in God's hand ... and God heard her prayer. A few hours later, Roger passed in his sleep. God took Roger's hand and and walked him into Eternity.

Some time after this, when Jen and I were on an airplane leaving for a much-needed vacation, I pulled out the book on prayer and had time to read it. I was hoping to glean insights and inspiration, something that would spark an understanding on prayer.

Instead, I read from this author's perspective about how he recommended different kinds of prayers to get what one wanted from God. It was based on the author's interpretation of Scripture, and had a bit of a "cake recipe" approach to prayer. It almost suggested that if a person does Step A, then you can expect God to do Step B, and so on. I did my best to read the book. I tried to stay open-minded, hoping for something of value; yet the more I read, the more it felt like a dry and formulaic procedure, to the point of sucking the heart right out of any prayer time with God. I didn't even bring that book back from vacation; it's somewhere strategically placed in the southern Caribbean.

Who would have known that the only inspiration I needed to write this part about prayer would come from the tender love and devotion of a daughter toward her father, and not from a scholarly book written by a "Biblical expert"? Prayer is as we are and just that — nothing more needs to be added or enhanced. Our prayers are from our hearts, however rough that may be at times. God hears, and He answers all.

Prayer is a Two-Way Communication With God

Read that again. How would you want to approach that for yourself? God will take you as you are, and in any way that you come to Him. He will accept you as you bring yourself to Him. He doesn't judge harshly, He won't be critical (even if you don't use a "prayer formula"), and He will understand not only what you are asking for but He also knows what you **need**, and He will arrange and organize the events of your life to be in your best interests, especially from an Eternal perspective.

Sometimes what we want and pray for will happen … but always when we pray, what we **need** will happen. God knows the difference, and He is gracious to provide for our needs.

*My God shall supply all your **needs**, according to His riches in glory, by Christ Jesus.*
Philippians 4:19; emphasis added

Given some experience in communication with God, when we are quiet and open, it is not uncommon for Him to speak to our hearts in His way. The ways we pray can be as different as we are diverse people: short, simple words … or longer, more detailed accounts. The breadth and depth of prayer varies, but what is always important is the condition of our hearts in the prayer.

Each night, before going to sleep, I pray; it is a version of this:

"Dear Father, thank You for the many blessings in our lives, those we know about and those we don't. Forgive us for anything we have done that was hurtful to You. Please bless Jack ... please bless Kael ... please bless Kyle ... please bless Alisa ... and bless Jen and me, and all our family and friends. Keep us close to You and close to each other. Bind any evil that would try to hurt us or our loved ones. Thank You for guiding us through the choices of each day, and using us to touch the lives of others."

Following that, I will often pray for more specific things, such as if there is a health challenge for someone ... or asking God to watch over all the students in our schools ... or praying for God's blessings for our ex-spouses ... or discussing with Him a big life decision or event coming up ... or simply lifting all the emotions and thoughts and questions and concerns I have about anything! I know that God is listening, and I am trusting through this prayer that He will help sort things out the way they are supposed to go. It's a trust thing, a close time with my Best Friend.

There have been times when something was on my heart for weeks or months, and it was like a theme which I persisted in prayer over a long time. Not because I doubted God's ability to deal with it — on the contrary! — **I persist *because* I trust in God's ability to deal with it!** Some areas of our lives touch our hearts so deeply; we have opinions and hopes and feelings, and they matter deeply to us. God is willing to listen, to share, and to stay engaged.

Clearly I recall the season of prayer over my son Kyle's college and career development. Part of his degree included work-based internships; he did not have a lot of experience in these, combined with being deaf, which makes communication more challenging. Kyle wanted to succeed in the hearing world, and to succeed in a very tough career of Chemical Engineering. So I was praying for God to help him on many fronts. God and I stayed on it together.

It was amazing to watch how God brought the first of four work-internships to Kyle. He landed in a company that prides itself on hiring people with disabilities, and then out-performing their competitors. Kyle was placed in a lab setting with another person who was deaf. It wasn't so much the work he did at that placement that pleased him, it was seeing another deaf person doing the work too that gave Kyle much-needed confidence.

His next work-placement was at a craft brewery, where he learned the challenges of a small company, the importance of having a profound work ethic, and the importance of bringing his best to the job every day. I was enjoying how God was answering my prayers by blessing my son!

The third placement gave Kyle more experience and confidence, and taught him about "economy of scale" in many ways. His last placement was with a large chemical company where — when he asked them for a challenging project — they gave him one that really pressed his capacities and capabilities, and resulted in a product enhancement that was actually used by the company.

Each of those placements were in the exact and perfect order for Kyle to develop competence and confidence. These were all answers to prayer that — even in my most profound love for Kyle — I could not have imagined or designed a better sequence or set of experiences. Why? Because God loves Kyle even more than I ever can.

After graduating, Kyle was hired into an entry-level job as a Chemical Engineer, and continues to grow and learn more about himself, about work, about people, and all that goes with living and taking care of yourself as a young adult out on his own. He is with the same company, has high-level security clearance, and is one of their top engineers.

When my daughter Alisa was going into 6th grade, I asked her what she might want to do as a career. Without hesitation, she said she wanted to be a Veterinarian and help animals. I said, "That is great, a Vet but not a Doctor who works with people?"

She answered, "I like animals better than people." And that was that. We started helping her get volunteer experiences at local Vet clinics, which turned into part-time summer jobs as she grew older. When she was in middle school, I e-mailed the School of Veterinary Medicine at Washington State University, and found a woman who would be a mentor for Alisa as she went through school, advising her on the correct classes to take, what experiences to look for, etc.

Interestingly enough, when Alisa graduated from Seattle Pacific University with a degree in Pre-Veterinary Medicine, she was accepted at WSU in the School of Veterinary Medicine. And who did she meet? The very person who had been her e-mail advisor for several years! That person, Barbara, was then retiring from WSU, but had a significant impact on my daughter's trajectory. It is so great when people who have climbed a career mountain, give advice to others wanting to follow that path.

My daughter was always driven and very capable, and still is today. She and her husband, who is also a veterinarian, are dedicated and talented in their work.

Once Alisa was taking a very challenging class called "Organic Chemistry"; she called me to say she was really struggling, and wondered if she should change her career choice. I listened, and asked her a few questions (mostly about what she really wanted). She wanted to be a veterinarian, but this one class was just really tough. Apparently, for anyone wanting to go into medicine, Organic Chemistry is kind of a "gatekeeper" experience.

I prayed while she was talking, asking for the wisdom to guide her. What came to me was this: "Alisa, if you want to be a veterinarian, stay with it; let's just figure out how to get you through this particular class." So she got a tutor, spent extra time doing labs, and working with her Professor. She earned a B in the class, and was on her way. You see, I didn't know what to say, how to support her, whether or not I should encourage her to opt out, or just to give her a pep talk — but God knew what she needed in that moment. All I did was ask Him.

I still pray for all my kids. Conversations with God (also known as "prayer") are ongoing, continuous, like old friends picking up where we left off last time. The point of this example is that God was answering my prayers for Kyle during his college and career life over five years! God's answers were better than anything I could have imagined, and showed an insight into what my son needed even more insightful than anything I could have designed. We need to trust that when we pray for something — and have an idea of how we think it should go — that God knows better than we do, and we need to accept that God is up to something, has something in mind, that is better than best!

My Racing Prayer

When I was racing, it was a lot of fun but also a bit scary at times, for a variety of reasons. Just before leaving the pit to enter the race-track, I developed a personal prayer; I prayed:

"Jesus, be with me / Jesus, be with me / Jesus, be with me / Jesus, be with me / Jesus, be with me"

The second part goes:

"Jesus is with me / Jesus is with me / Jesus is with me / Jesus is with me / Jesus is with me."

Then we — Jesus and me — would go racing! During the race, I was never afraid. I was calm, clear and focused, and — as fast as the car was going — it was almost like slow-motion because my mind was processing everything in real time. It was a very different setting, and it was a different kind of prayer.

Not because of any formula, but because that was what I needed to connect with God in that moment.

Is it possible to be legitimately praying, interacting with God, while driving a race-car on the track? Absolutely! We change the timing, the format, the approach to prayer, not because of what God needs but because it is what we need. Look at how Jesus advised us to pray; the beautiful "Lord's Prayer" cited in Matthew 6:

> *"Our Father in Heaven, hallowed be Your Name. Your Kingdom come, Your will be done, on Earth as it is in Heaven. Give us this day our daily bread; and forgive us our debts, as we also have forgiven our debtors. And lead us not into temptation, but deliver us from evil."*
>
> **Matthew 6:9-13**

We are to ask God to accomplish His will in our lives and, yes, to ask for those things we need, as simple as our daily food. He encourages us to seek forgiveness, and to give forgiveness to others (who maybe don't deserve it — but we didn't deserve it either but receive God's forgiveness out of His mercy and grace).

Remember: there **is** Evil, and we are to ask God to help keep us safe from it, and not to be led into it. And, make no mistake, God does not *"lead us into evil or temptation"*; we can wander into it easily enough on our own. It's not so much that we don't have the "fire insurance" through Christ, but because when we give into temptation, we are giving evil power over us. That can take us off the path we want to be on with God …

and it will require God's forgiveness to get us back on track.

Over the years, I have prayed for simple, daily things, and for complex life things: prayed for others who were sick ... asked God to reveal an answer or truth in various situations ... prayed when I was happy, sad, content, afraid, confident, restless ... prayed when I was exhausted, and simply saw myself laying on my face, with my arms wrapped around the feet the Jesus. I have prayed in all things, and in ways that have never ceased in my life. [37]

And I will be praying when I pass from this Life into Eternity, knowing I don't deserve a place in Heaven but still believing on the Name of Jesus for that exact promise to happen!

---

[37] See 1st Thessalonians 5:17.

Chapter 25: **GOD IN THE STORM**

After months of prayer and reflection, in July 2016, I retired from 32 years in public Education. I had spent 22 years as a public school superintendent. I feel blessed to have served in my career, and God used me to make a positive different. Still, in my heart and mind, I knew it was time for me to transition to the next stage of my life. I now do Leadership Coaching and Consulting, but only as much as I want. I have been enjoying having more time to do other things.

My wife and I always enjoyed our friends and the community up north, where we would visit often, and we felt like it would be a great place to raise our children. So we bought a home and moved to Lynden, Washington. It has been a great decision as we really enjoy the community and life here. We are just a few minutes from the Canadian Border, in Whatcom County.

A Healthy Community

My retirement has been being able to spend more time with my family, helping coach some of my boys' teams, enjoying hobbies and activities, as well as supporting my wife with more help around the house. She is still working at a local Elementary school. Jen is the Dean of Students, and has such a gift for working with people. My stepsons are fully involved in school and Sports. They are neat people. It was great that their Dad also moved to the area, to stay involved in their lives.

We got connected to a local church here, *North County Christ the King Community Church,* in Lynden, Washington. We really like the pastors, the staff and the people there. When COVID-19 hit our area — as it did around the world — and, with my cancer treatments, we had to shift to attending "online services." However, as things are moving forward, we have been able to make more in-person connections with people.

This community has a great many churches, and the concept and practices of people living their faith in God is abundant. Still, like anywhere else, there are people who seem genuine in sharing God's love … and there are some who appear to think they are "better than others," based on how they interpret the Bible. I pretty much try to stay out of the doctrinal differences that some churches promote, and think it is better to simply follow the greatest commandment: to love God, love others, love yourself. It is, and will be, God's decision through Jesus as to who gets into His Kingdom at the end of time. I do not feel qualified, nor do I want to assume or make distinctions about those decisions.

There are public schools here that our boys attend, with many great teachers, coaches and staff. A number of them are Christians, and thus far, the sharing of faith in various settings is very open. There is also a large Christian private school in the community, and some people choose to send their students there. I still feel that having everyone together in a public school system is best, for the reasons I shared earlier in this book. However, I can see, in some instances, where a parent's decision to have their student attend in the private setting was good for those students.

Overall, the relationship between people in the community, public and private schools alike, is mostly respectful. There are frequent athletic games between the public and private schools, and they make for interesting and healthy competitions.

Like everywhere else in our country, there are strong political opinions and differences between people, in about every organization. As a thinking person, I have my own thoughts and opinions, I mostly feel called to share God's love above the debates, and for all people, right, left, middle, etc. **I believe that for many, "being strong" on their issues is such a prevailing wind in their minds that they don't feel God's breath on their hearts to love others.** It is nearly impossible to untangle these things with people; we can only love as God calls us, and hope that they can see more clearly from their hearts as time passes.

First Signs

In the summer of 2020, we were enjoying family time, and even made a trip to North Dakota for my wife to see her grandmother before she passed. I was fully engaged in water-skiing with my friends, and for the most part, life was rolling along great.

About three weeks into August, I was having severe pain in my upper abdomen. After three days of this, we figured it best to go see our family doctor, Robin Caldwell. We made an appointment and, given the description of symptoms, they got me right in.

The doctor spent five minutes with me, and then said, "You need to drive to the ER at the hospital right now." My wife drove me, and soon I was being admitted and scanned, to see what was happening. My skin was also turning yellow, which was because my biliary tract (the drain for the liver) was blocked. After more tests and such, the medical conclusion was that I had advanced pancreatic cancer. There was a tumor in the tail of my pancreas which had invaded my spleen; and another tumor on the Biliary tract, which was blocking it. So they did temporary stents to open the biliary tract, and gave me medicine to deal with the pain and such. Then I was discharged to go home and take the next steps: connecting with cancer doctors.

We decided to contact and work with *Seattle Cancer Care Alliance* (SCCA); and doctors at the University of Washington who specialize in treating these things, who have an excellent reputation. We knew it was a serious type of cancer.

After consulting with the doctors assigned to my case, in September 2020 I started treatments. It is a hard thing to be told you have cancer of any type, and is particularly difficult when it is **advanced pancreatic cancer, that is likely not curable.** So the treatments I have been doing are for **Life Extension.**

As of right now (March 2022), **19 months ago, the original prognosis was that I had 6 to 12 months to live.**

From a faith-based perspective, I was still in the hospital in August, praying and asking God what was happening. He said, *"Not to worry, Nick. You are secure in this life, and in the next. Simply do your best, share your faith along the way."* So that is what I did, and that is what I am doing.

Sharing Reality

I do not have Social Media accounts. With my Leadership Consulting work, I did set up a *LinkedIn* profile, which allows people to interact with me. To "share my faith," I decided to use my *LinkedIn* account to share posts that update people on medical stuff, as well as how I was leaning into my faith in God on the cancer journey. I figured it appropriate for "leaders" to see how a person faces and deals with life challenges.

I started posting right away, back when things started in 2020, and am continuing to post updates now. As I worked with my editor to get this book launched, we simply thought it best to bring you, the Reader, these posts in the order in which I wrote them. These posts, as of the completion of this book, are printed in the next chapter. Assuming I am still here after you read this book, you are most welcome to send me a connection request and follow along on this journey; or just visit my *LinkedIn* page to read the posts. It has been helpful to read the replies, prayers, support, and encouragement from people; I wish we had time to include them all too!

I pray that you will find something helpful in your life by reading about my journey ... mostly that in so doing, you will be drawn closer to God in your heart in some way. That is my hope for you!

~ 2020 ~

Peace In the Storm

Hey, all! After a trip to the Emergency Room on August 24th, nearly a week of in-hospital tests and procedures, I have cancer leading into my liver, which came from a tumor on my pancreas — thus, Stage 4 pancreatic cancer, as it has already spread.

I will be working through the Seattle Cancer Care Alliance [SCCA] for treatments. I will be in good hands. In our joined hospital room last week, I shared with a 20-year-old recovering from a collapsed lung: *"God is always up to something. And while there is always the pain, the fears, the unknowns, the challenges of the immediacy of our situations, if we step back — take a moment and reflect —we will realize that* **we are, and it is, all in His hands.** *We do our best, and trust Him for the rest."*

There is peace in the storm if we look to God rather than focus on the storm. While God doesn't cause these things to happen, He can use us in these moments to impact others. I prayed with the young man and gave him encouragement before I left.

Sorry, this isn't a post about a kitten doing something cute or funny — but it is what it is. This is life. Thanks in advance for prayers. I'll give it my best!

[Often in response to inquiries from friends, Nick added further details; here as "Post Scripts." — **Editor]**

Post Script: Apparently the cancer is too advanced for surgery at this point, so I will do chemo first, probably starting next week. Then see how it responds, etc. ... Turns out I have a mass on my pancreas, which they think spread to the liver. But the first symptoms were liver-related. Anyway, now the doctors have the target, so onward to treatment. ... They got biopsy material from the mass on the pancreas this morning. So that should help them "aim" my next steps.

Stay At It!

Thanks for the many who have offered prayers, love and support. The doctor updated us today, based on the results of the recent biopsy. I have pancreatic cancer that has spread to the liver. The best course of treatment will be chemo first, not surgery. I will connect with the SCCA oncologist next week, and start the chemo battle as soon as the doctor says to do so.

As I have shared with some already, often we don't get to pick our situations. Still, we can pick our attitude, perspective, faith, etc., in those moments. I have always faced my challenges. I don't run, avoid or complain. My strength comes from my relationship with God, and it isn't shaken by things that happen to me.

My long-term outcome is secured by the gift of life Christ made possible. I don't know when that day will come, but will humbly accept His grace and go forward when it does. Rest assured, I am not one to give up if something is hard. I will do my best to beat this, or at least extend my life to be with my family and friends, and do whatever God wants me to do while I am still here.

A sincere thanks for your prayers and words of encouragement. Stay busy, using your life well, doing positive things for all of those around you. Stay at it, my friends! God bless and keep us always!

Post Script: Not the best news, still I am going to do my best to work with the doctors and try to extend my life. But when God calls me home ... then it is onward, and I am at peace about all that stuff.

110% Effort

Hi, all! First off, a sincere thanks for the prayers, support and encouragement these recent weeks. It has been a lot to process, for sure.

So today I had my long meeting with the oncologists at SCCA. I have pancreatic cancer that is at Stage 4, because it has metastasized to my liver. Thus, if I sought no treatment, the average survival projection is six months. With chemo — and assuming chemo works — the projected average life span goes up to one year, maybe more if I respond really well. I also signed up for a clinical trial that has both chemo and immunotherapy drugs. I will find out next week if I get into that. Treatments will be at SCCA.

For sure, I am going to go through chemo and do my 110% best to extend my time with family and friends … but I am also getting things in order, to help my family in the future. As I have said all along, I am close to God and know that — even though I can't always see, understand or make sense out of some things — He always loves and holds me. I will probably do another update in a month or so, to let folks know how the chemo is going. Keep making a positive difference with your life. Blessings always!

When Things Get Tough

Hi, all! So, Sunday through Tuesday of this week was rough. Had to have the stents in my liver duct replaced; one was clogged. Then spent the night in hospital recovering from the related infection and pain. The pain feels like the scene from the 1979 *Alien* movie, where the creature pops out of one's upper abdomen. By Wednesday morning, was well enough to have my port replacement. Yesterday and today, brought much needed rest at home.

Good news: my blood test results have me qualifying for the clinical trial at SCCA. It is a mix of immunotherapy and chemo. The first round starts next week.

I am humbled by the prayers and support from everyone — God bless you all! My son flew home to spend time together. It has been great to see him and have those meaningful talks about the uncertainty of the near future; but, in God's grace, the certainty of Eternal Life. I can't remember the movie, but there was this great line about how *"When things get tough"* — I mean, really tough, and you don't know if you are going to make it ... you don't give up. Because you can live with living, and you live Eternally if you die ... but if you give up, you get nothing. So onward, folks! Keep loving! And never throw in the towel — use it to wipe your tears. Keep your arms wrapped around the feet of Jesus, and press on!

Staying Motivated

Introducing my son to one of my dearest friends; so they now have each other in their lives going forward.

My body is now having symptoms from all the treatments. Blood tests show the stents in my liver are holding, which is good. I am walking two miles every day, but too fatigued to continue weight-lifting mixed with some cross-training on the in-between days, so I am adjusting. Not much appetite, so making myself eat per schedule and staying within one pound of where I was a month ago.

It feels better bringing the fight to the cancer now! Thank you all for the prayers and encouragement. It really helps me stay motivated. We pray from our hearts for what we want to happen — God hears our prayers, and answers with what is best for us, for others, and the infinite perspective. However, our prayers and His plans align ... and we need to trust Him for the answers that are in everyone's best interests. Blessings always!

Post Script: Chip is a man of God and a close friend who has promised to keep my son Kyle under his wing, if or when the day comes and I am not as immediately available. They have bonded right away, and launched their own relationship. Kyle is 32 and very successfully employed as a Chemical Engineer; is also DHH, and benefits from having a good life sounding-board/coach from time to time. I have always felt honored to be that person for Kyle; so with my new reality and various outcomes possible, I just want to make sure he has that with someone I trust with him, going forward.

Miracles Welcome!

Hi, all! Thank you for the prayers and encouragement you have given in this cancer battle. It helps more than you may know.

The weekly chemo infusions continue to go as planned; some bumpy "symptoms" days, but mostly manageable. Jen (my wife) is so supportive, with a loving strength.

I have enjoyed select visitors in recent weeks, and soulful conversations with friends along this path. The possibility of Death sure puts Life into perspective.

Today, as I sat at SCCA for my infusion, it was tough to see so many young people from all walks of Life going through treatments too. Cancer doesn't discriminate.

Treatments will continue, and at the end of November, the doctor scheduled a CT scan to see how the treatments are impacting my cancer. Please pray it is being effective and our goal of life extension is making progress. Miracles welcome!

In all of this, my prayers are known by God. My only qualification is that His will being done is the most important will of all.

I can't even put into words my gratitude for you — those I know and those of you I don't — offering your love on this journey. May God bless and keep us all, always.

Post Script: While I know that I am forgiven by the grace of Christ, lately I have been struggling with some fear of the unknown. It is like I have faith in my head but not fully in my emotions (if that makes sense).

> *The LORD is compassionate and merciful [kind], slow to get angry, and filled with unfailing love. ... For His unfailing love toward those who fear Him is as great as the height of the Heavens above the Earth.*
>
> **Psalm 34:8, 11**

The timing of the Scripture, *"The LORD is kind"* (Psalm 34:8) is helpful. Because when I pass, I will need His kindness. ... God sustains us; and each of us can bring His love and voice to others by being available to Him and being present with others. My thanks to so many for bringing His love and voice to me on this journey. I am developing the opinion that in our Lord's Prayer, where it says, *"Thy Kingdom come,"* each of us has a part in bringing that Kingdom to others, in our words and actions.

Positive Impact

We met with the SCCA oncologist and reviewed the results of the November 30th CT scan. Based on all the information, the first two months of treatments thus far are having a positive impact on the cancer.

We thank God. And thank you for your prayers and encouragement in this journey.

Today I start Cycle 3 Infusions through December, with Cycle 4 set for January. The next CT scan will be at the end of January. Thanks again for your prayers; keep them coming! Blessings always.

Post Script: We are in University of Washington hospital now, more complex situation. Big decision tomorrow. I know God has this in His plans. Still, prayers welcome.

We Are Not God!

We can become more effective leaders in our work, but we won't be perfect. Our careers and lives will always have a mixture of success and hardships. That's Life.

In the Bible, in the book of Job, God allows hardships in the successful life of Job — not as a punishment, but rather to show that Job is truly a good person of faith, and not one who is only successful due to Life's circumstances.

Yet, when things are really rough for Job, he — and those around him — begin to question, *"Why, God?"* After a time of silence, God engages Job, not with direct answers to how Job framed his questions to God but, rather, God poses questions **to** Job, which actually were affirming God's sovereignty, wisdom, capacity, love for His children, and so on — all of which are beyond our comprehension. Do we know how to make a world, or to fully understand or explain the reason for suffering? God is reminding us that He is God ... and we are not!

We must recognize human limits, and trust God will take care of what we (and others) cannot know or do. We need to embrace good and hard times without full understanding, and lean into God through prayer, faith, trust, hope, and love. We need to stop expecting Eternal answers regarding Infinite truths during our mortal and temporal time in this Life. We are not God! I, for one, am glad of this.

Mountain Tops Or Valleys

I was feeling better after the last CT scan the first week of December, and that week's doctor meeting. Since December 9th, my last infusion, we were cautiously optimistic about progress. Then Friday, December 11th, 2020, I had no energy, was running a fever, feeling dehydrated. We called the after-hours SCCA nurse/doctor support-line. They sent us to ER for blood tests, etc.

The next day, they found a bacterial infection in my blood and a severely inflamed gall bladder, so had me come back to hospital. In addition to strong IV antibiotics, they placed a drain through my liver into the gall bladder, to let it drain. As I am in Bellingham hospital, I had the doctor here speak with an SCCA doctor on call for my team. He concurred with placing the drain. That was done this morning, December 12th, 2020.

While the procedure went as planned, it hurts like *^&% having a five-inch needle poking into your side. So now sorting out how to move, to deal with it, etc. I know there are people who have it worse, but for sure this has been — and is — quite a journey for us. Can't even find the words to thank you all for the loving, earnest prayers and encouragement you provide. You keep my head above water as Jesus holds my heart. Mountain tops or valleys — God is with us! Stay firm in your faith, my extended loved ones.

Post Script: I got out of hospital for Christmas with my family, which was nice. I am working with my doctors to resume treatments, and then deal with the gall bladder stuff. ... They transferred me to the U of W hospital yesterday. Doctors trying to figure out how to deal with two different bacterial infections, bad gall bladder, and abscesses on my liver — all in the context of my Oncology treatments. But they seem smart, and I still got fight, so onward!

Staying Vertical

After 8 days of IV antibiotics, the drain still in my gall bladder, and my vitals and blood cultures stable, the doctors let me go home for Christmas. The medical journey continues after this week; still, I am so grateful to have this time at home.

My sister called and shared about her friend and his cancer battle, but without the hope through faith of life after this life. I can't imagine how alone he must feel, and offered to visit with him.

You see, it is about the vertical: staying alive and upright! For those who believe in and, yes, are saved by the gift of Jesus given to us, the "vertical" continues after this life. In addition to sustaining us in this life, we have God's promise of Eternal Life beyond. In His love, we have life and hope and a future. When worldly props are gone, where will you turn?

Thank you again for your ongoing love, support and encouragement. I am human too; there were three times I wept this week: when they took me by ambulance to another hospital, where my wife couldn't visit … when I thought I may not live to see my family again … and when I wondered how steep this hill is, and if I could make the climb. But those tears passed as I leaned into my Lord and waited for His presence.

May you find peace and joy this Christmas and always!

Onward!

Recently in my cancer battle and facing mortality, I was wrestling with feelings of not being worthy, not good enough for Heaven. I know I am "saved" in a soul-sense through Christ, but was caught up reflecting on (feeling) my shortcomings. Earnestly I prayed and, then, listened. In a firm voice, God said, *"I am not going to call you out."* [38] I asked for understanding.

Calling me out for my sins — which are already forgiven by Jesus' actions — would be drawing attention to them, rather than my soul entering as a result of the Eternal Life made possible by Jesus' sacrifice. What Jesus did is more important than what I did wrong — my repentance from my sins make it possible for me to accept His forgiveness.

Salvation is ours through God's grace, not our good works, nor is it thwarted by our sins. God wasn't saying I was perfect, nor was He scolding me; rather, He was strongly re-affirming that I am forgiven and being accepted in His eyes by what His Son did for me. **I *feel* the message now, not just in my head — I understand it in my heart!**

I am forgiven to the extent that me sharing on this journey has value! My friends, we have been set free! We have to choose to accept His forgiveness and leave the self-imposed "prisons" we create, often in our own hearts and minds. At times, Leadership is seeing and accepting things that fall outside our normal perspective; it is seeing with new eyes. Blessings! Onward!

---

[38] See Psalm 103:12; also Romans 5:8

~ 2021 ~

Lighting A Candle In A Cave

This month I got through my infusions without symptoms causing me to end up in the hospital. Next, I go for an ultrasound of my gall bladder, and CT to see if treatments are working.

With such a change in my health, I have moments when I question my value; at times, feeling more of a burden than asset. I suspect these feelings are normal for people in my situation. Still, they don't make the journey easier. So I just pray through them, and then God has a person light a candle in my cave with a message or a call. In this light, I have had wonderful visits and enjoy these connections.

Just yesterday, one of my neighbors sent a text. He is in his 70s, in the hospital with COVID-19, fighting for his life. He wanted me to call and pray for him. It was my honor. So it seems, in ways we don't always plan or appreciate, God will still use us, finding value in loving on others. This assumes we are available for His purpose, and not too busy or distracted in our own stuff.

Thank you who have continued to reach out, sent prayers and encouragement. God continues to hold my heart and soul — but it is the kindness of your support that keeps my head from hitting the cave walls. May God lead us to His Kingdom. Blessings!

Reading "Travel Guides For Heaven"

We got updates from the doctors of my recent scans. The tumor is stable. It is good that it isn't growing or spreading, but I am not a surgical candidate at this time. The plan is to continue treatments.

I have one of two rare situations in that it is either:

(A) Pancreatic cancer, spread to the biliary tract of the liver. If so, surgery not ever an option. Prognosis is about 16 months.

Or —

(B) Pancreatic cancer, and a different cancer on the biliary tract. If so, surgery may be an option if neither of them grow or spread in the next few months. Prognosis — and if I survive surgery — pushes out to five years.

So it is what it is, and I am in good spirits, marching forward. I am reading some books on Heaven. I figure if there are travel guides, I ought to study up a bit (LOL). I continue to appreciate the prayers, love and encouragement from all of you. It is only by the grace and strength of God that I am getting through this — but isn't that the truth for all of us, and our many different challenges of Life?

When our lives get hard, lean into God! And if you need someone to listen or pray with you, just let me know. I want to be of value and used by God. Love and blessings!

Post Script: The process has been quite challenging; still, in it all, God is sustaining me. Ultimately I trust Him for the outcome. ... I feel like most days I am keeping a good attitude, but confess I have been so active before cancer that now, I just can't do the workouts, the skiing, the house projects, etc., that I want to do. So I do what I can and lean into God. ... Had yet another hospital stay over the weekend, home now and trying to recover enough for my next infusion this week. Good words from friends help me on this journey.

Remind People To Be Kind

Hi, all! I hope this finds you well. Each day, with more sunlight, welcomes the promise of Spring, May God's love and light lead us!

My last infusion was February 5th; my liver enzymes were too high for treatment, so we will try again next week. Doctors are not sure why, but it may be a response to immunotherapy.

Speaking of health providers, one of my doctors replies to e-mails even on weekends, is super communicative and is just the best! My nurses everywhere have been awesome! Still, I had one provider make a comment that the patients she sees usually don't live very long; and on another visit said not to bother her with questions unless it was during a planned visit, as it takes away from her time. So, I am keeping the doctors and the nice people on my team, but requested not to see her (*"Nurse Ratched,"* for those who remember *"One Flew Over the Cuckoo's Nest"*) anymore. If you are a leader, remind people to be kind to others!

I am feeling okay, but need to get back to treatments. My gall bladder drain is misbehaving, so will get that addressed too. These are just sort of my "new normals" (LOL).

I had a dream the other night in which I was in the most beautiful place. I wondered if God was giving me a glimpse?

Thanks always for your prayers and support!

Post Script: This place in my dream was soooo cool! It was a beautiful lake and Infinity Pool-type edges, made of smooth rock, so the water gently curled at the edges. On one side, lush green plants, trees, etc.; and on the other side, snow-covered land forms. I was in the water; it was warm, just the right temperature. I was first exploring the cliff formations, then wading in the water. One of my best friends was there. I was physically strong again, but still me. It was a skiable lake, but I didn't spot a boat (LOL). There was a beautiful house sitting on a hill looking over the lake. There were also a few other people there, one of whom was giving me a little tour. In my mind, I was wondering if it was public or private property. Afterwards, what came to me was that it wasn't public or private — it was shared by anyone who was there.

Sunshine and Rain

Our lives are sunshine and rain. When we are in God's care, both serve our best interests. Embrace!

Elevated liver enzymes that thwarted treatments in February are back in normal ranges, so I made all of my March infusions. My next CT will help us figure out progress.

God is shifting my perspective from being *"a living person facing death"* to *"a person who is going to pass but is facing life here longer and then a better Life Eternally."* It may be a distinction that makes no sense to some, but it changes one's outlook to *"living Life to its fullest,"* not fearing death, and knowing the future is secure in His plans! I am going for it!

My peace comes from God. My life and purpose will go on ... just in a different Place. I am humbled and grateful for this gift, made possible through Jesus, blessed by God our Father, and led by the Holy Spirit.

So yes, I am doing my best with my stuff here and now. My prayers are for His strength to do my part well, loving others, and being available for His use. May His will be done!

A heartfelt thanks for your continued prayers and encouragement. It makes a positive difference to feel you with me; it keeps wind in my sails and my boat heading into this storm. I am not alone. God bless you always!

Spring Has Sprung

This week's CT scan showed the tumor size the same, and nothing new. The radiologist's terms were "stable" and "unremarkable," which at first made me think it was a personality test (LOL). So treatments continue, and our goal of Life Extension is advanced.

There was an interesting reflective moment after the scan and before the results. I wondered, *"Will things be better or worse?"* Then my mind went to: *"Well, in light of more time in this life, or going to Heaven, which results would be better or worse?"* Then I felt, *"Well, more time in this life or moving closer to Heaven are both great outcomes."* So there it is — and there I am!

I am at peace in God's hands, happy Spring has sprung and I'm doing my best to share God's Love and Light, in hopes others will move in His direction.

Again, my heartfelt thanks for your prayers and encouragement. It is hard to find words — you see, much of the time, many of the days each month, the physical symptoms are so draining ... thus, your contacts are like emotional flowers that live in me.

I know this life — passing at some point — and my Eternal Life, my future, is solid. Thanks be to the Lord and Savior! On this journey, your presence with me is so precious! Thank you for your kindness and love.

Seeing Beyond

After my ERCP yesterday, I developed a fever of 103.5 F and am back in the hospital. IV antibiotics brought my temperature back to normal; however, liver function numbers are not where they need to be able to go home.

Yesterday, after all the ER intake work was done, I had a long time waiting for a room to open. These experiences, while not my preference, cause me to pause and reflect. During this time, all I wanted was Jesus.

Understand, I am not one who sprinkles His Name around like seasoning salt. Often I am offended by how His Name is used so casually by people. But on this journey of mine, my greatest blessing has been — and is — the gift of knowing Him better.

I never know now which "next" medical event will be my last, or how many days I really have left. Yet, even in the middle of these medical events, with all the unknowns, He is with me, protecting my heart, reassuring and helping me see beyond the immediacy of my situation.

So tomorrow is Easter. Please reflect for yourself — and help those around you to appreciate — Jesus defeating Death, rising to New Life, and it's significance for all who call on Him, who will also rise and live beyond this Earthly life. Really get to know Him in this life! Carry His Light and Love with you!

Thanks always for your prayers and encouragement. Happy Easter! God bless!

Post Script: The doctor let me leave the hospital Easter evening. The liver numbers trending down. Just happy to be home, resting up, then back for chemo on April 14th. ... I have more blood tests today, oral antibiotics and, IMHO, need some days to recharge, before reporting back for more treatments. God is always up to something; we just need to pray and trust Him for all things.

Connected to God

After reviewing my current medical situation with my doctors, we have set mid-May for surgery to remove the tumor on the tail of my pancreas and spleen, and trim any impacted areas of my stomach and colon. The gall bladder will also come out. The tumor on my biliary tract will just have to wait its turn.

After I recover from surgery, the biliary stuff will get targeted therapy until/if a point comes when we can reconstruct the biliary tract. Apparently, the two metal stents keeping me alive, also make that surgery more difficult. Oh well, I have a great doctor, good medical insurance — and Heaven on the other side!

With this planned surgery, I get a break from chemo, so felt good enough to go with my family to someplace warm! God's creations are so beautiful; it is easy to see how we can get lost in the things of this world, and forget developing relationships with our Creator!

So, **the "secret recipe" to Christian-based leadership is to be connected to God through the gift of the Holy Spirit,** Who gives us His guidance and the words to say, in each unique situation. We just have to be willing to put down our agendas, and be open and available for His.

Thanks for your continued prayers, support and encouragement. Blessings!

Post Script: In Christ, we have already won. This life is in His promise, and within the context of Eternal Life. … God asked me to share on this journey, so I'm just being obedient in His light. Trusting Him for life now, however, longer, and Life Eternally, in His timing.

God's Exchange System

Yesterday, I had a 10-plus hour surgery. The doctor removed the tail of my pancreas, my spleen, gall bladder, and small areas on my stomach and colon. Today, I am in recovery, getting "things" to function again, managing pain with a hydromorphone pump, and using ice (old school). I did 6 laps around the floor, dragging my IV pole (LOL); I will do 3 more laps by the end of the day = 1 mile.

I have great nurses; got to visiting with some and prayed with two. One was questioning her value after 37 years as a nurse; and another who felt stressed balancing her family, attending nursing school and doing her hospital practice time.

I have enjoyed and been enriched by texts from family and friends. And just two days ago, the hospital changed its Visitors Policy, to allow one per day — my wife volunteered for that place!

The sun is out, I see water from my room, and though my surgical areas remind me I am not poolside, I am at peace in God's hands. God brings us to others and brings others to us. Be available. Keep your heart open to those "in line with you," and share His love with others.

Thanks again for your prayers and encouragement. You make me feel valued and cared about. I am keeping my eyes off my predicament and fixed on doing His work.

Post Script: I did chemotherapy and immunotherapy from September 2020 to April 2021 at SCCA. Yes, not fun at all. But it stabilized the tumor such that I could have this surgery. I have another, different cancer on my biliary tract; we will address it after I recover. So, miles to go. Close to God every step.

Endurance and Trust

After meeting with my oncologist, here is a new medical plan going forward. Continue my post-op recovery for another 4 weeks, then start a treatment plan that includes "biliary tract stent cleaning with radio frequency ablation" (ERCP). This will happen every few months to keep the plumbing open from my Liver and try to address the tumor on the biliary tract.

I will also resume chemo on an every-other-week basis, to seek to address cancer cells in general; however, we will delete the experimental drugs I was taking for the first 8 months of my treatment. Based on where I am now after surgery, the doctor couldn't make a case to continue the experimental drugs, given my type of cancer; they created havoc with my body, and were pretty high risk.

The goal of life extension is still the aim; but we are trying to include "quality of life" as a factor too, and not be so aggressive that treatments kill me before the cancer (LOL). My wife and I feel this plan is the right next steps on this journey. I value her love and strength.

While I am spiritually very secure, at peace and deep in God's loving arms, the physical recovery from surgery has been slower and less comfortable than I expected. Thus, a good portion of the time, it has taken my all just to manage. But each day is a little better, so I think it is just enduring, and leaning forward, and letting time happen.

When a person isn't able to do what they used to do, it begins to erode your sense of value in your own eyes. So positive contacts help keep one's perspective in a healthier place. I have been pretty independent and self-sufficient in my life. Thus, in this journey, I have really come to appreciate the prayers and support from others. Thank you!

Life right now is trying keep my eyes on helping those around me, trusting God with everything, and doing my best each day. May God bless and keep you.

Thanks, Chip!

There is no greater love than to lay down one's life for one's friends.

John 15:13

While this Scripture at times, for some, has meant actually giving one's life, it also includes those sacrifices made to be there for a friend. In this light, I want to publicly thank Chip Kimball, my friend. For several months, Chip volunteered to drive to my house to get me, then drive me down to chemo at SCCA, staying with me through the infusions, and then driving me home. This gave my wife a break too.

His support, conversation, faith, humor, kindness, and love were so powerful, and brightened me on what were otherwise "cloudy" days. I suspect the in-person razzing he and I exchanged was at least somewhat entertaining for the nurses (LOL).

Chip leaves soon to his new role as Superintendent of an International school. I will miss my friend. He showed me "the power of one"! May God grant us the capacity to lay down our busy lives for others, in the way Chip has modeled so brilliantly in mine. May God bless and closely keep him and his family as they travel, and he begins to work abroad.

To Chip: It was great having Kyle go with me, as he came this week to hang out. Still, I couldn't help think about all our great times together as you went with me to SCCA last winter. Since I chose not to be in the Phase One Trial now post-op, they are infusing me on the 7th floor, not the 5th; in the same room where they do the blood work and health review pre-fusion. It was a new model and way better. We drove the car we got for Kael (a Kia "Soul") to test it out on the long drive, and that being the same, your "boxy clown car" at least made me feel a little better (LOL). I was impressed with how well it does in all types of driving. Let's see: looks bad but feels good … what is it? Anyway, get busy there in Prague, as I know they will value you as a person and a great leader. God has you too, my friend.

To other friends: In your daily contact with staff, students and parents, God's light in your eyes, in the tone of your voice, in your expressions, in the care and competence — these are reflecting in real time God's love for people. Draw strength from Him, and then just share it! This helps draw others closer to God. Just share it! … Can't imagine how a person keeps above water in these things without faith in God. Life and death of one's body, while sobering, doesn't compare to not feeling Eternal Love in one's soul via grace, hope and faith in God. That's where my real life is, where my treasure is. Still, will keep doing my best to stay vertical in his life, knowing that vertical orientation remains in the next, thank God. … Today was my first chemo in three-plus months. Let's see how I look at the end of September (LOL)!

Giving With A Cheerful Heart

We wanted to get away before the next series of procedures, so we enjoyed time at Suncadia. We walked down to the river, which meant walking back up from the river too. There are benches every few flights, so I took breaks long enough to catch my breath but not so long as to attract hungry mountain lions.

Since my May 13th surgery, I am feeling better; yet don't have the physical strength or endurance I want back. So, started physical therapy on July 15th to get structured help to enhance my quality of life. We will see if I can keep it up once chemo starts up again. I had another CT on July 9th and an ERCP and RFA on July 12th. Chemo is to resume later in July or August. The doctor wants to try every other week for awhile, so we will give that a go.

Recently I was praying about the concept of giving money in a Christian way, and wanting to honor God in the same. A couple days later in a dream, I felt this overwhelming emotion in the Spirit, with the message being God wants us to have a cheerful heart when we give, and not do so out of a dry sense of duty. Waiting on the Spirit to lead or inspire to give seems key, as is walking in the Spirit so we are responsive.

Thank you for your continued prayers, support and encouragement. God bless!

Post Script: I believe people should be "real" and not "pose" — the same being true for any aspiring to lead others.

"My Own Movie"

I was watching an old movie with a great cast of actors, each playing their role well. Since that production, one has passed, and others have had great careers but are not featured much these days. As they worked together in their time, they were engaged in the story they were telling.

Isn't this true for all of us? Still?

Each of us brings our self to the production of life stories with other characters. Perhaps with family, friends, work colleagues, or even strangers — but in each act, we are uniquely assembled for reasons, perhaps beyond understanding at the time. We are interconnected to the life stories of those around us.

How do we play our part? Our roles may change, but the camera of life is still rolling. Our eternal relevance isn't measured by the size of our audience, but rather by how well we reflect God's love to whomever is in our story.

Can we realize the larger design of life, and appreciate how our life — our words and actions — impacts the lives of others? Can we see with gratitude how others shape or influence us? Do we see ourselves as God sees us, as the unique treasure we are in His eyes and in His heart? Can we love God, ourselves and **all** others? Can we see the bigger picture, and not be overwhelmed by temporary scenes?

We are each given one life … it is **our** movie. May God help us to be our best in the roles we play, and trust Him beyond our part.

When I was diagnosed in August 2020 — prognosis: *"6 months to a year"* — one of my goals was to live long enough to dance with my wife at our friend's wedding. That was about a year ago, and, by the grace of God, we danced! Now, after months of chemo, a 10-plus hours surgery, multiple ER trips and procedures, I am still vertical as I head into this next year. Yes, it will be a year with more chemo and more procedures, but these are just more "short scenes" in "my movie" — these are not my life.

I am thankful that all this has drawn me closer to God, and given me an "Eternal Life" perspective of what really matters, especially in the context of so much that doesn't matter. May you really know and experience God in your life!

Strong Enough to Pray

I hope this finds you well and enjoying summer. It's been so nice in the Pacific Northwest; we have been able to enjoy outside activities. It has been so dry, some days we wish we would get a little rain!

As you can see from the picture, my post-op recovery is complete, and now I am back in the chemo "saddle" again at SCCA. Today was my first chemo in three-plus months; I may not look as tanned and with hair at the end of September (LOL).

My oncologist has prescribed three chemo treatments each for August and September. Then, depending on my October 6th CT, I may get time off! I will still be having ERCP and RFA on the stents in my biliary tract to keep the plumbing open and treat whatever is happening in that area. I am getting used to these procedures and — since I die if I don't do them — figure I will keep doing them (LOL).

So far, I have been able to do PT, and am exercising to keep my body moving towards strength rather than weakness. Though, in Christ, I am strong regardless of my physical condition.

I am so blessed by the continued prayers and encouragement from my family and friends — that includes you! Thank you! I am in God's presence in all of this, and trust Him.

I volunteered to be in an inter-church Prayer Booth at the Western Washington Fair in Lynden, Washington, on August 12th, from 1pm to 7pm, and again on August 19th, from 10am to 4pm. If you are in the area, stop by to enjoy the Fair, and come visit me at the Prayer Booth — and let's pray! And for those not Fair-bound, if you ever want me to lift you in prayer for anything, just message me. I want to support you on your journey too.

Blessings! Onward!

Post Script: Into week 2 of 3 with this month's round of chemo, and the treatment symptoms came back in full force. ... I was doing okay Monday and Tuesday, but since Wednesday my body hasn't been at all happy: fatigue, nauseous, belly drama, you know — all the fun stuff. ... When we consider there are both more stars and more planets in the Universe than grains of sand on all the beaches in our world, and more molecules in ten drops of water than all the sand on our world, it makes one ponder and thoughtfully consider just how unique we are as God created us. He has got us — well, those of us who chose to be gotten — through the grace of Jesus.

We All Need A Hug

Today I met with the oncologist at SCCA to review the recent CT and blood work, and discuss our next steps. He wants me to do three more chemo sessions this month, and then stop treatments for three months, coming back in January with another CT to evaluate progress. I will still have an ERCP mid-November to keep my liver stents clear, and draining, which I accept as my "new normal."

At the end of the meeting with my doctor today, we had both just said our farewells, when suddenly he was standing facing me, with both arms open to his side. I thought this was kind of odd, so I sort of squinted my eyes as if to say, *"What?"*

This made him say, "What?" ... and I said, "You look like you want a hug."

He laughed and said, "Sure, let's hug," so we gave it the *"casual guy to guy side hug,"* both laughing as we did. Then he said, "My shoulder has been bugging me, so I'm just stretching." Oh well, it was funny, and a good ending to what are mostly serious discussions.

I have been doing my PT, exercising to try to get back strength. I am slowly making progress. This past weekend, I was outside doing some yard work and pressure-washing. I should have listened to my body and just called it done when I was tired. However, a neighbor offered me space in his utility trailer for yard-waste.

Not wanting to pass that up, I got out my chainsaw and went after this large limb on one of our trees. I cut it down, but as I was chopping it into smaller sections, I literally had to "take a knee" from being light-headed and out of energy. I couldn't even pull the cord to start the chainsaw, or lift it anymore.

My neighbor and his wife, seeing this fatigue coming over me, took the chainsaw, cut up the limb, loaded it into the truck — all the while telling me to just rest. As humbling as it is for me to not be able to do as much work as I expect from myself, it is even more heart-warming to be surrounded by such kind people.

When we make ourselves available to show God's love to others, everyone is blessed. Thank you again for your continued prayers, love and support on this journey! May God bless and keep you always … and picture: Chemo attacking cancer cells!

"I Will Still Be Holding Your Hands"

Picture an ant protesting a passing train: *"But I had plans! I had plans!"* But my plans were set aside as I had an "urgent" ERCP to clear the stents in my biliary tract. The procedure went well.

I reported to SCCA for my third round of this month's chemo, and my liver enzymes were way out of range. These numbers — and, well, just really awful symptoms — set off the appropriate response from my medical team. So my plans of working in the Prayer Booth at the Fair this week did not happen. I made it last week for part of my shift, but it was 101F that day so they sent me home early. And — so sweet! — my 15 year-old step-son said he wanted to go to support me, in case I needed help. He stayed with me the whole time! And my older son flew from Virginia to support me two weeks ago. Precious hearts!

Three weeks ago (before chemo resumed), I was feeling good ... and had this dream:

> *I am back in college, anxious about turning in a paper about surviving my greatest challenge. I finished the paper and am on my way to turn it in ("old school" = in person), and wondering if I should drop the class due to being in treatments, etc. Anyway, I get to the Teacher and reach out with both hands to hand in my paper ... but He doesn't take my paper at first — He holds my hands. The Teacher is Jesus!*

> *He says, "It doesn't matter if you drop the Class for grade or credit. I am going to take you through the lessons I have planned." He adds,*

"And you will pass and with a good grade, and when it gets really hard, I will still be holding your hands and get your through those parts." *Then He says, "Let's see what you wrote."* *(In addition to the profound, He always shares a bit of humor; it does wonders for my perspective.)*

Anyway … that was three weeks ago, when I was feeling good. Before this ERCP, I could hardly get out of bed from being weak. **I leaned on His promise, trusting Him to get me through.** And even though plans changed, I followed.

"My thoughts are nothing like your thoughts," *says the LORD," and My ways are far beyond anything you could imagine. For just as the Heavens are higher than the Earth, so are My ways higher than your ways and My thoughts higher than your thoughts."*
                                              Isaiah 55:8-9; NLT

If you would, please include my wife, daughter and father-in-law in your prayers. My wife is a year out of back surgery, but recent tests suggest her pain and numbness may require further surgery. My daughter just got released from the hospital following a major surgery. And my father-in-law is still in ICU from a major surgery over a week ago. I'm not sure if this is some type of modern-day Job (from the Old Testament), but just in case, pray that if there is a quota of medical crap as part of this "test," it be shifted off my family and onto me. I can take it — and its pains — better than if and when my loved ones are impacted.

Okay, folks, not meaning to dampen your Inbox ... just giving an update, and hoping the next one is more fun! Blessings!

Post Script: The ERCP was this morning, and my stents were clogged. After the cleaning procedure and a quick recovery, they sent me home. So I'm hoping to feel better in a couple of days. Also, my daughter was released from her own hospital stay and is at home, doing fine. But my father-in-law, who was in ICU, passed away a few days later. God bless you and those who lifted him in prayer. ... It's like swimming in a lap-pool; I keep hitting the walls, but just turn and swim some more. You guys are helping with my emotional buoyancy!

Extra Innings

So this week I had my third chemo infusion for this month. Now I get three months off, with a CT on January 7th to see if there is any recurrence. On the liver side, I am scheduled to have my biliary stents cleaned mid-November. Chemo symptoms this month are not fun, but I expected the same and now am just taking it one day at a time. The three months off of treatments will be nice, and help me to be more active as I feel better.

I continue to be humbled by the prayers, support and encouragement from people — even those I don't know from our *LinkedIn* community. Given I am now living in extra innings (based on my original prognosis), the prayers must be influencing God's plan in all of this, to keep me here longer. I am trying to do my best with the opportunity.

A couple of weeks ago, I was musing about how I can live with living or passing, but this fence of "the unknown" was, well, uncomfortable. I am sort of an *"If we are going to do something, let's get to it"* person. So I realized I needed to just exercise my gift of free will and decide, *"I am going to live like I am going to live, rather than sit around wondering."* It is amazing how fast that perspective got me to engage again, in a good way.

As Viktor Frankl wrote so eloquently in his book *"Man's Search For Meaning"* [39]: *"When all else is taken away, the only thing we can control is our attitude."* I

---

continue to feel God's presence in my life. My walk with Him has an emotional intimacy I have never felt before. In truth, I am more curious than anxious about my future. Each day, I am available to be used by Him in some meaningful way.

God's Glory is a Light House for us who — in the fog of our own agendas — risk running our lives onto the rocks. May we keep His Light in our eyes and hearts, and live in accord. Blessings!

Speaking At A Christian Business Leadership Conference

Hi all. I am one of the guest speakers at "*Illuminate*," a Christian Business Leadership Conference coming up on Thursday, November 18. It will be at the *Christ the King Church* in Bellingham, Washington. I am thankful to be feeling well enough to participate. Thank you for your continued prayers and support on this journey. May God use me in any way to draw people closer to Him. Blessings!

God's Big Picture

Since my last post, I have had two ERCPs (one urgent, one scheduled) to clean out the metal stents in my biliary tract. These are necessary life-extension procedures.

After 10 months of chemo, I have been on a chemo break since September, and pretty well recovered from the 10+ hours surgery mid-May. My next CT is in January, to see if there is any recurrence. I have been trying to exercise in order to overcome neuropathy, and be as active as I can. God willing, my physical goal is to water-ski again this spring/summer.

Given a chemo break and clean stents, I am helping my mother-in-law get her motor-home to Arizona. It is a welcome break from our PNW cold and rain. [Note: my sunny picture at the Orange Grove RV Park in Bakersfield, California; just ate an orange right off a tree — yummy!]

My speaking engagement at a Leadership Conference last month went well. God has been leading, supporting and teaching me. I praise Him. And, while I am glad to be in extra innings from a medical prognoses perspective, I am also ready anytime God wants to bring me Home. His will be done! I just want to be useful in His eyes.

Some years ago, my son came home from college, distraught from a recent break-up. After listening and empathizing, I got a long tape-measure from my toolbox. I asked him to tell me in inches how long would be a good life. He paused, and replied, "90 inches."

I said, "Okay, show me where you are now by age on this tape." He did. I said, "Point to this exact time, this moment of real sadness of the breakup." He did. I said, "Not wanting to disregard the real sadness you feel now, how does it measure up in the entirety of your life?"

He reflected, "It isn't very big when seen over the whole thing."

Then I said, "Now look at your life from an Eternal perspective, as it exists in God's Kingdom." How long would this 'Life' tape measure be?"

He thought and said, "It would wrap around the Earth and go on, forever."

I shared how — if we choose God — then He uses our lives here to teach and shape us into our Eternal selves. "As hard as this break-up is now, it is teaching you about yourself, about relationships, life, and so on, which will help you in the long run. **Rather than focus on this pain, ask God for relief, strength and wisdom."** In this light, experiences we have which are really hard should be viewed as our "teachable moments" from an Eternal perspective. God's Big Picture is true reality for us — beyond our "90 inches" or however many years we are granted.

Family, friends and *LinkedIn* colleagues — thank you for your prayers and encouragement over this last year and a half. As I am now into my 63rd "inch," you have been so kind. If I can support you in any way, please message me. I appreciate you, and pray that **God's love will fill your hearts this season so that you**

will have no option but to overflow the same to those around you! Take care. I will post another update after the January chemotherapy. Blessings!

~ 2022 ~

"Peaceful On Purpose"

With my cancer journey, I have been trying to explain to people how a person can be at peace and have hope, in the midst of really hard circumstances. I came across a book that explains Biblically how and why we can be at peace and see hope in the midst of things. I just finished reading *"Peaceful On Purpose"* by Joel Osteen, [40] and recommend it for those who believe in a God Who loves you and is bigger and greater than your problems. Blessings!

---

[40] *"Peaceful On Purpose: The Power to Remain Calm, Strong and Confident in Every Season"* by Joel Osteen; copyright 2021; published by FaithWords.

"The Life We Have Been Given"

We spent today at SCCA. They did blood work and a CT. The radiologist saw an area of concern near the pancreatic cancer surgical site that, when viewed in light of the blood work (elevated CA-19 9) — could be recurrence of cancer. However, another part of the blood test (elevated Alkaline Phosphotate) showed my biliary stents are clogging again, which could make the CA-19 9 tumor marker high for non-cancerous reasons.

So, my oncologist wants me to get my stents cleaned, and see if they can get a biopsy of the concerning area. Blood work will be repeated in a couple of weeks, to see if the CA-19 9 marker has changed. If data shows cancer is growing again, then a PET scan will be done and treatment options reviewed. If not, then I get another 3 months before they scan again.

The other day, I was musing about how I didn't make the decision to be born. Mind you, I am happy to be here; still, it wasn't by my hands. The gift of Life was and is God's design. So it follows that the timing of passing from this life to the next is also His to make, not mine. **What is ours is what we choose to do with the life we have been given.**

My prayer isn't for specifics; rather, simply for His will to be done with me — and that I can do my best with my part. To worry about that which I cannot control is a waste of energy. With faith, hope and trust in God, I am continuing to focus on that which matters, and thankful to be within His loving plan.

Thank you so much for your continued prayers and support. I appreciate you!

Listen, America!

We need to **deeply listen** to views and interests that may be difficult to hear, may be different than our own. So often people label, or name-call, or dismiss others who see things differently! We are all in this Life together, and need "others" to be successful too. We cannot reach common ground by imposing our positions.

I challenge political leaders, and you in leadership positions, to **schedule Deep Listening Tours.** Invite the "others" and don't use it as an opportunity to make your case — rather, just listen, ask questions, to understand more deeply. Thank people for sharing. And when you go off to consider leadership actions, for the greater good, remember to include those "others" and their needs or interests as much as possible in moving forward.

There is too much presenting of positions, and not enough listening to fully understand the diversity of needs and issues of "others.." Imagine Media hosting Deep Listening forums, where leaders of our states and country come to listen to all Americans, and not to talk to their special-interest groups.

Listen, America!

God Sees Differently

Based on recent tests, my doctors conclude that the cancer has recurred. Since I have been dealing with advanced pancreatic cancer, a recurrence was expected. It is now impacting an adrenal gland, my stomach, my colon, a kidney, and my lymph nodes. This week, we discussed treatment options: more likely more chemo and/or another surgery.

In joking with my doctor, I suggested I should have brought my Black Labrador dog Stella to the "PET" Scan. He replied, "If they don't think it's funny, just tell them that she is your Therapy animal." Or I could say she is there for her "Lab" work (LOL)!

This last year and a half has included 10 months of chemo, 8 months of Immunotherapy, numerous ERCPs, dozens of ER visits, endless CT scans and blood draws and hospital stays, and a ten-plus hours-long surgery. While I appreciate there are ways to extend Life, more treatments and their side-effects will be challenging. However, I have made a family commitment to live as long as possible, so I will move forward and not complain.

I am trying to stay balanced by staying alive and living my life. I may take a break from treatments this spring or summer, to be strong enough to water-ski a bit — that's a short-term goal. **Long-term: when this body doesn't work anymore, God has a Heavenly body waiting! I am looking forward to that in time.**

Miracles still happen when they are within God's plans. Still curious, I was praying and asking God why there aren't more people with health or physical challenges healed. *"Why aren't they fixed?"* I mused.

He answered: *"Because they are not broken."* **The way God sees us is very different than how we see people.** God sees our hearts and souls!

This journey has drawn me closer to God, and for that strengthening, I am deeply grateful. And perhaps, because I've been sharing along the way, others are also leaning into Him more.

A question here: When Jesus, dying on the cross, says, *"Father, forgive them, for they know not what they do"* (see Luke 23:34) — who are "them" and "they"? Was Jesus asking His Father to forgive just those people standing around the cross at that time … or, for the "them" and "they" throughout the ages who still do not know what they do?

I am very thankful for your prayers and humbled by your support. Blessings always!

Post Script: It has been an interesting journey, for sure. I just talked with my doctors regarding my treatment plan. I start chemo (*folfirinox*) on February 15th; then again every other week for three months, leading up to CT and PET scans. Apparently, this is a very strong chemo regimen, so need to put on my big-boy pants! … I understand about Life seeming unfair when we view things like this from our Earthly perspective. Clearly in that light, there are those who have it worse than me, better, etc. But my life has always had — and still does have — a purpose greater than me, one in which our Heavenly Father has used me and others in meaningful ways. This cancer situation is within that scope as well. While realistic about my prognosis, I am optimistic about Eternity through Christ's gift and our Father's grace. So onward! And yes, if I can, I will ski more while I am still here. … Talking with my doctors on Tuesday to figure out a plan that, yes, gives me a window this spring/summer to ski, God willing!

Another Cowboy In Heaven

Thank you to all who have been keeping me company over the last year and a half. I appreciate you, more than words! You bless me and keep some wind beneath my wings.

Four days ago, my wife and I snuck away for a half-day of snow-skiing. We rested as I needed and stayed on easy runs; still, it was just nice to get up to the mountain, enjoy God's gift of beauty and sunshine, and to be together.

Today I am back at SCCA, starting another round of chemo. This time it is *folfirinox,* a stronger mix as the pancreatic cancer has returned (as expected). Anyway, as I have been doing, I will do my best and trust God for the rest! His love sustains!

About the question regarding forgiveness that I posed in my last post: I believe Jesus will determine who qualifies, and at what threshold of "belief" to meet His criteria to get into Heaven. I am not suggesting everyone gets in, but I think He is more forgiving than we understand.

One of my older brothers, Sam, passed away a month ago; he had a serious mental health issue in his adult life. It caused him to not be able to process things at all. He also was really hard to be around; at times he was cruel, even to my oldest brother Doug, who graciously cared for him. Then Sam would return and be remorseful. He was tormented in ways.

Sam simply did not have the mental capacity to process — let alone pass — the typical prayer for salvation. There are many people who today, don't know what they do. Sam was one of them.

An older sibling was concerned that Sam hadn't prayed the way it was thought he should to secure his salvation; however, I think he did as a child, before the mental health stuff exploded and messed up his functioning.

I took this to God in prayer, asking Him about Sam ... and I felt that God said He understood Sam. God knew all about Sam's mental health limitations, and He was going to take care of him. I shared this with my siblings: ***"God knows Sam, and will find him a good horse, an open range, a camp fire, and friendship in his place in Heaven."*** A couple of days before he passed, Sam reached out to me (he wouldn't let anyone visit him in hospice), and I shared with him this picture of him in Heaven.

Thanks again for your prayers and encouragement.

Chapter 26: **GIVING YOUR LIFE TO GOD**

None of us are capable of living our lives on our own power and making everything work out well. We are not God, so we need to stop acting like we are.

We are flesh and blood, and mortal, and may do great things and may do awful things. We may be right in some of our thinking, and we may be wrong at times too. We are human.

We should approach life as a gift, keep things in perspective, and be kind to others — even those people we may not like or agree with. And — news flash! — our current bodies are not going to last forever on this Earth. Yep, we are all going to face the big What's Next after this life. If you want your heart, soul and personality to live forever, you need to make some choices in the here and now.

There are many different views on the big What's Next. It can be confusing. There are metaphysical, and philosophical, and theological, and religious, and scientific, and mythological opinions over generations about the existence and meaning of Life. It is understandably challenging to sort through it all, and make sense out of our place, in this massive Story of Life, from one generation to the next.

I am only an expert on what I have experienced in my life. I can only share with you my truths. You must spend the time to figure these things out on your own.

Here are my parting words for you.

To My Christian Family

If you are a Christian, pray that God's Voice, through the Holy Spirit, will become stronger in you and lead you, drawing you closer to the heart of God. Learn to see through the eyes of your heart. Learn to get quiet in the midst of this busy, fast-paced world we live in. Maybe try setting down your phone for a while. Learn to lay down your ego, your agenda, and your busy self ... so you can be still and learn to hear and recognize God's Voice.

Pray for God's will to be done, and that you can do your part. Our time on this Earth is really short compared to Eternity, so get busy with what God wants you to do: loving people from your heart. And please, if this applies to you: stop doing and saying things (even religious things) in the Name of God that are not from God, and have the effect of turning people off about what it means to be a Christian.

Who did Jesus come to save, who did He have compassion for ... and would you let those people in your church? Who were the religious experts of Jesus' time that really made Him angry? Who are you, really, as a Christian, and how do others "experience you"?

For My Other Dear Friends

If you are not a Christian, and don't know God, Jesus and the Holy Spirit in a personal way ... just pray in an honest, heartfelt, sincere way, asking God to come into your life. This prayer usually includes asking God to forgive us for our screw-ups, and knowing that

— through the life, death and resurrection of Jesus —
this forgiveness and new life are possible.

It is a gift of grace — yep, we don't deserve it, and
we can't earn it — it is profoundly a gift from God
through His Son's work on our behalf. Make that
choice to invite God into your heart. After this prayer,
start connecting with people who are living and loving
from a God-centered, faith-based way, and get busy
doing the same with your life.

While I have read many books, I still find the Bible
to be the most powerful way to get to know God, Jesus,
and have it influence one's perspective in helpful ways.
If you are new to this, start by reading the Gospels (the
first four books of the New Testament), and pay
attention to what Jesus is saying and doing! While it is
good to get connected with people who can help
answer questions, and come alongside you as you
move forward in Jesus' way, **don't depend on other
people for your faith in God. Let God develop your
relationship with Him** through honest prayer, and take
fully the guidance of the Holy Spirit God will put into
you! Walking with God becomes like breathing: you
just open, and He fills you!

Epilogue

I don't really know how many days I have left on
this Earth. While I am continuing to do my best in my
medical challenges, I really am at peace knowing my
What's Next is secure in God's hands. I trust Him more
than I trust myself, or any other person on this Earth.

So that's my story ... and I pray you find Him, or
invite Him, into your story as well.

My friends: love God, love others, and love yourself — and in so doing, you will live a life of meaning and purpose, as we are called to do by our Creator. And yes, **love the people in line!** I hope to see you later … maybe in this life, or on the other side. God bless us always!

Nick

ABOUT THE AUTHOR

Dr. Nicholas Brossoit was born the youngest of six children, in Ephrata, Washington. He enjoyed playing sports, spending time with his friends, and exploring a variety of hobbies and interests. He graduated from high school and accepted a full scholarship to play college Football, first at *Washington State University* and then at *Pacific Lutheran University.* He graduated from PLU in 1983, with a Bachelor of Education Degree and Teaching Credentials.

Nick worked as a teacher and coach at *Peninsula High School,* while also earning his Master's Degree and Principal's Certification at PLU. He was hired and worked as an assistant principal at *Burlington-Edison High School,* before transitioning to a District Administration position. During his 7 years in that District, he was encouraged to get his Doctorate. He earned a Doctorate in Educational Leadership, with Superintendent Credentials, from *Seattle University.* In 1994, Nick was hired as the Superintendent of the *Tumwater School District,* near the State capitol of Olympia, Washington. He served in that role for 10 years. In 2004, Nick accepted the job of

Superintendent of the *Edmonds School District,* and worked there for 12 years.

He retired in 2016, having spent 32 years in Public Education. Nick is considered among the most effective school leaders to have served in Washington State. Many of his innovations and leadership actions still resonate. He is a gifted public speaker who could take complex issues and share them in ways that people could understand.

For several years, he served as president of an organization that successfully sued the State of Washington to increase public school funding. Nick always deferred the credit for accomplishments to others, whom he said were part of the "team" that made positive things happen. In his career, he led efforts in raising over $1-billion for school operations and capitol improvements.

Upon retirement in 2016, Nick helped to coach his stepsons' Sports teams, and still enjoys recreation and hobbies with his family in the Pacific Northwest. His family is connected to the *North County Christ the King Community Church,* located in Lynden, Washington.

Nick and his first wife, Joyce, have two grown children: Alisa, who is a Veterinarian; and Kyle, who is a Chemical Engineer. Joyce remarried, and works as a District Administrator. She and Nick have an enduring friendship; he credits her for being a wonderful mother to their children, and he values her forgiveness for choices in that marriage he says he should have made differently.

In 2010, Nick married Jennifer Vachon, and enjoys being a stepdad to Kael and Jack, both now high school student athletes. Jennifer works in Public Education as a Dean of Students at a local elementary School. Nick says she is one of the most loving and strongest women he has ever known. They have a dog, Stella, who barks way too much, and two spoiled cats, Cedar and Caesar.

For more information or inquiries, contact: **njbrossoit@gmail.com**

INQUIRIES

For more information or inquiries, contact: **njbrossoit@gmail.com.**

BULK PURCHASES

For more information about purchasing bulk quantities, please contact: **jeannehalsey@mac.com.**

Pay It Forward

When I *get* this book, I will buy one and *give* it to another, as inspired!

CPSIA information can be obtained
at www.ICGtesting.com
Printed in the USA
LVHW050933130422
715980LV00010B/452